I0121179

Felix Octavius Carr Darley, John Townsend Trowbridge

The Drummer Boy

A Story of Burnside's Expedition

Felix Octavius Carr Darley, John Townsend Trowbridge

The Drummer Boy
A Story of Burnside's Expedition

ISBN/EAN: 9783337329631

Printed in Europe, USA, Canada, Australia, Japan

Cover: Foto ©Thomas Meinert / pixelio.de

More available books at **www.hansebooks.com**

THE

DRUMMER-BOY

THE

DRUMMER BOY.

A STORY OF BURNSIDE'S EXPEDITION.

BY THE AUTHOR OF "FATHER BRIGHTHOPES."

———————

BOSTON:

PUBLISHED BY J. E. TILTON & CO.

1863.

Entered, according to Act of Congress, in the year 1863, by

J. E. TILTON & CO.,

In the Clerk's Office of the District Court of the District of Massachusetts.

STEREOTYPED AT THE

BOSTON STEREOTYPE FOUNDRY.

CONTENTS.

(3)

4 CONTENTS.

THE DRUMMER BOY.

I.

FRANK AT HOME.

ONE evening, in the month of October, 1861, the Manly family were gathered together in their little sitting-room, discussing a question of the most serious importance to all of them, and to Frank in particular. Mrs. Manly sat by the table, pretending to sew; but now and then the tears rushed into her eyes, and dropped upon her work, in spite of all she could do to keep them back. Frank watched her with a swelling breast, sorry to see his mother so grieved, and yet glad in one little corner of his heart; for, although she had declared that she could not think of granting his request, he knew well, by those tears of hers, that she was already thinking of granting it.

"A pretty soldier you'll make, Frank!" said Helen, his elder sister, laughing at his ambition. "You never fired a gun in your life; and if you should see a rebel, you wouldn't know which end of the gun to point at him, you'd be so frightened."

"Yes, I know it," retorted Frank, stoutly, determined not to be dissuaded from his purpose either by entreaties or ridicule; "and for that reason I am going to enlist as a drummer boy."

"Well," exclaimed Helen, "your hands will tremble so, no doubt you can roll the drumsticks admirably."

"Yes, to be sure," replied Frank, with a meaning smile; for he thought within himself, "If she really thinks I am such a coward, never mind; she'll learn better some day."

"O, don't go to war, dear Frank," pleaded, in a low, sweet voice, his younger sister, little Hattie, the invalid, who lay upon the lounge, listening with painful interest to the conversation; "do, brother, stay at home with me."

That affectionate appeal touched the boy's heart more deeply than his mother's tears, his elder sister's ridicule, and his father's opposition, all combined. He knelt down by little Hattie's side, put his arms about her neck, and kissed her.

"But somebody must go and fight, little sister," he said, as soon as he could choke back his tears. "The rebels are trying to overthrow the government; and you wouldn't keep me at home — would

you? — when it needs the services of every true
patriot?"

"Which of the newspapers did you get that speech
out of?" asked Helen. "If Jeff Davis could hear
you, I think he'd give up the Confederacy at once.
He would say, 'It's no use, since Young America
has spoken.'"

"Yes; like the coon in the tree, when he saw
Colonel Crockett taking aim at him," added Frank:
"says the coon, 'Don't shoot! If it's you, colonel, I'll
come down!' And I tell ye," cried the boy, enthusiastically, "there's something besides a joke in it.
Jeff 'll be glad to come down out of his tree, before we hang him on it."

"But if you go to war, Frank," exclaimed the little
invalid, from her pillow, "you will be shot."

"I expect to be shot at a few times," he replied;
"but every man that's shot at isn't shot, sissy; and
every man that's shot isn't killed; and every man
that's killed isn't dead — if what the Bible says is
true."

"O my son," said Mrs. Manly, regarding him with
affectionate earnestness, "do you know what you say?
have you considered it well?"

"Yes," said Frank, "I've thought it all over. It
hasn't been out of my thoughts, day or night, this
ever so long; though I was determined not to open

my lips about it to any one, till my mind was made up. I know five or six that have enlisted, and I'm just as well able to serve my country as any of them. I believe I can go through all the hardships any of them can. And though Helen laughs at me now for a coward, before I've been in a fight, she won't laugh at me afterwards." But here the lad's voice broke, and he dashed a tear from his eye.

"No, no, Frank," said Helen, remorsefully, thinking suddenly of those whose brothers have gone forth bravely to battle, and never come home again. And she saw in imagination her own dear, brave, loving brother carried bleeding from the field, his bright, handsome face deathly pale, the eyes that now beamed so hopefully and tenderly, closing — perhaps forever. "Forgive my jokes, Frank; but you are too young to go to war. We have lost one brother by secession, and we can't afford to lose another."

She alluded to George, the oldest of the children, who had been several years in the Carolinas; who had married a wife there, and become a slave-owner; and who, when the war broke out, forgot his native north, and the free institutions under which he had been bred, to side with the south and slavery. This had proved a source of deep grief to his parents; not because the pecuniary support they had derived from him, up to the fall of Fort Sumter, was now cut off, greatly to their distress, — for they were poor, — but because, when he saw the Union flag fall at Charleston, he had written home that it was a glorious sight; and they knew that the love of his wife, and the love of his property, had made him a traitor to his country.

"If I've a brother enlisted on the wrong side," said Frank, "so much the more reason that I should enlist on the right side. And I am not so young but that I can be doing something for my country, and something for you here at home, at the same time. If I volunteer, you will be allowed state aid, and I mean to send home all my pay, to the last dollar. I wish you would tell me, father, that I can have your consent."

Mr. Manly sat in his easy-chair, with his legs crossed, his hands pressed together, and his head sunk upon his breast. For a long time he had not spoken. He was a feeble man, who had not succeeded well in the business of life; his great fault being that he always relied too much upon others, and not enough upon himself. The result was, that his wife had become more the head of the family than he was, and every important question of this kind, as Frank well knew, was referred to her for decision.

"O, I don't know, I don't know, my son," Mr. Manly groaned; and, uncrossing his legs, he crossed them again in another posture. "I have said all I can; now you must talk with your mother."

"There, mother," said Frank, who had got the answer he expected, and now proceeded to make good use of it; "father is willing, you see. All I want now is for you to say yes. I must go and enlist to-morrow, if I mean to get into the same company with the other boys; and I'm sure you'd rather I'd go with the fellows I know, than with strangers. We are going to befriend each other, and stand by each other to the last."

"Some of them, I am afraid, are not such persons as I would wish to have you on very intimate terms with, any where, my child," answered Mrs. Manly; "for there is one danger I should dread for you worse than the chances of the battle-field."

"What's that?"

"That you might be led away by bad company. To have you become corrupted by their evil influences — to know that my boy was no longer the pure, truthful child he was; that he would blush to have his sisters know his habits and companions; to see him come home, if he ever does, reckless and dissipated — O, I could endure any thing, even his death, better than that."

"Well," exclaimed Frank, filled with pain, almost with indignation, at the thought of any one, especially his mother, suspecting him of such baseness; "there's one thing — you shall hear of my death, before you hear of my drinking, or gambling, or swearing, or any thing of the kind. I promise you that."

"Where is your Testament, my son?" asked his mother.

"Here it is."

"Have you a pencil?"

"He may take mine," said Hattie.

"Now write on this blank leaf what you have just promised."

Mrs. Manly spoke with a solemn and tender earnestness which made Frank tremble, as he obeyed; for he felt now that her consent was certain, and that the words he was writing were a sacred pledge.

"Now read what you have written, so that we can all hear what you promise, and remember it when you are away."

After some bashful hesitation, Frank took courage, and read. A long silence followed. Little Hattie on the lounge was crying.

"But you ought to keep this — for I make the promise to you," he said, reflecting that he had used his own Testament to write in.

"No, you are to keep it," said his mother, "for I'm afraid we shall remember your promise a great deal better than you will."

"No, you won't!" cried Frank, full of resolution. "I shall keep that promise to the letter."

Mrs. Manly took the Testament, read over the pledge carefully, and wrote under it a little prayer.

"Now," said she, "go to your room, and read there what I have written. Then go to bed, and try to sleep. We all need rest — for to-morrow."

"O! and you give your consent?"

"My son," said Mrs. Manly, holding his hand, and looking into his face with affectionate, misty eyes, "it is right that you should do something for your family, for we need your help. Your little sister is sick, your father is feeble, and I — my hand may fail any day. And it is right that you should wish to do something for your country; and, but that you are so young, so very young, I should not have opposed you at all. As it is, I shall not oppose you any more. Think of it well, if you have not done so already. Consider the hardships, the dangers — every thing. Then decide for yourself. I intrust you, I give you into the hands of our heavenly Father."

She folded him to her heart, kissing him and weeping. Frank then kissed his sisters good-night, his resolution almost failing him, and his heart almost bursting with the thought that this might be the last evening he would ever be with them, or kiss them good-night.

II.

OFF TO THE WAR.

It was a calm, clear October night. The moonlight streamed through the window of Frank's room, as he lay in bed, thinking of the evening that was past, and of the morning that was to come. Little Willie, his younger brother, was sleeping sweetly at his side. He had heard his sisters come up stairs and go to bed in the room next to his; and they were conversing now in low tones, — about him he was sure.

Would he ever sleep in that nice warm bed again? Would he ever again fold dear little Willie in his arms, and feel his dewy cheek against his own, as he did now? What was the future that awaited him? Who would fill his mother's place when he was gone from her? He had read over the prayer she wrote for him; it was still fresh in his thoughts, and he repeated it now to himself in the silence of the moonlit chamber.

When he opened his eyes, he saw a white shape enter softly and approach his bedside. There it stood in the moonlight, white and still. Was it a ghost? Was it an angel? Frank was not afraid.

"Mother!"

"Are you awake, my darling?"

"O, yes, mother. I haven't slept at all."

"I didn't mean to awake you, if you were asleep," she said, kneeling down beside him. "But I could not sleep; and I thought I would come and look at you, and kiss you once more; for perhaps I shall never see you in your bed again."

"O, mother, don't talk so. I hope I shall be spared to you a long, long time yet."

"I hope you will; but we must think of the worst, and be prepared for it, my son. If it is God's will, I can give you up. And you — you must make up your mind to brave all dangers, even to die, if necessary. It is a great and holy cause you are engaging in. It is no gay and pleasant adventure, as perhaps you think. Are you sure you have thought of it well?"

"I have," responded Frank. "I am going; and I am going to do my duty, whatever it is. For a few minutes after I came to bed, thinking of what you had said, and of leaving you, and of"—here he choked — "I was almost sorry I had said a word about going; it looked so dreary and sad to me. But I said my prayers, and now I feel better about it. I don't think any thing can shake my resolution again."

"If it is so," replied his mother, "I have nothing more to say." And she kissed him, and gave him plentiful good advice, and finally prayed with him, kneeling by his bedside.

"O, don't go, mother," said Frank; "it is such a comfort to have you here! May-be it is the last time."

"May-be it is, my son. But I must bid you good-night. You must sleep. See how soundly Willie is sleeping all this time! He don't know that he is losing a brother."

After she was gone, Frank felt more lonesome than ever, the house was so silent, the moonshine in his chamber was so cold. But he hugged his warm little brother close to his heart, and cried very softly, if he cried at all.

I do not know how much he slept that night. No doubt his excited thoughts kept him awake until very late, for he was fast asleep the next morning when Helen came to call him.

"Hurrah!" he exclaimed, starting up; "fight for the old flag!" for he was dreaming of a battle. "Hallo!" he said, rubbing his eyes open. "That you, Helen?"

"A wide-awake drummer boy you are," she replied, with her usual good-natured irony. "You'll have to rouse up earlier than this, I tell you, if you ever beat the reveille for the soldiers."

"So much the more reason why I should have a good nap in the morning, when I can," said Frank.

"Well, lie and sleep, if you want to," she added, with a touch of tenderness. "I thought I'd let you know breakfast was ready."

But Frank was wide awake enough now. He felt there was something great and grand in the day before him, and he was anxious to meet it. He was up and dressed in a minute. He threw open his window, and looked away towards the city, which lay dim and strange in the beautiful mists of the morning, with the crimson clouds of the sunrise lifting like curtains behind it. And the far-off roar of the rumbling streets reached his ear, inspiring him freshly with hope and action.

All the family were at breakfast, except Hattie, the sick one, when Frank came down stairs. Even Willie had crept out of bed before him, wondering what made his brother sleep so long that morning. And now he found the little fellow dividing his attentions between his breakfast and his toy gun, which had acquired a new interest in his eyes since Helen had told him Frank was going to the war.

"I'm going with my bwother Fwank," he declared, shouldering arms over his johnny-cake. "And if any body — any webel" — breathing earnestly — "Hurt my bwother Fwank, me shoot 'em, me will!"

"Yes," remarked Helen, "you and Frank will put down the rebellion, I've not the least doubt."

This was meant for a sly hit at Frank's youthful patriotism; but Willie took it quite seriously.

"Yes," he lisped; "me and Fwank — we put down the webellion. Take aim!"—pointing his toy at his father's nose. "Fire! bang! See, me kill a webel."

"How little the child realizes what it is to fight the rebels," said his mother, with a sigh.

"I'm afraid," said Helen, "Frank doesn't realize it much more than Willie does. He has just about as correct a notion about putting down the *webellion*."

"Very likely," said Frank, who had learned that the best way to treat a joke of this kind is always to humor it, instead of being offended. For a joke is often like a little barking dog — perfectly harmless, if you pass serenely by without noticing it, or if you just say, "Poor fellow! brave dog!" and pat its neck; but which, if you get angry and raise your stick, will worry you all the more for your trouble, and perhaps be provoked to bite.

There was a silence of several minutes — Willie alone manifesting a desire to keep up the conversation on war matters. He stuck his johnny-cake on the end of his gun, and bombarded his mother's coffee-cup with it; and was about to procure more johnny-cake, in order to shell the sugar-bowl, which he called

2

"Fort Sumter," when Helen put an end to his sport
by disarming him.

"I want father to go to town with me, to the
recruiting office," said Frank; "for I don't suppose I
will be accepted, unless he does."

That sounded like proceeding at once to business,
which Mr. Manly never liked to do. He was one of
those easily discouraged men, whose rule is always to
postpone until to-morrow what they are not absolutely obliged to do to-day. He waited, however, as
usual, to hear what his wife would say to the proposition, before expressing himself decidedly against it.
Fortunately, Mrs. Manly had energy and self-reliance
enough for both.

"If you are still firmly resolved to go, then your
father will go with you to the recruiting office," she
said; and that settled it: for Frank was resolved—
his character resembling his mother's in respect to
energy and determination.

Accordingly, after breakfast, Mr. Manly, with fre-
quent sighs of foreboding and discouragement, made
a lather, honed his razor, and shaved himself, preparatory to a visit to town. Frank, in the mean while,
made ready for his departure. He put in order the
personal effects which he intended to leave at home,
and packed into a bundle the few things he purposed
to take with him. An hour passed quickly away, with

all its busy preparations, consultations, and leave-takings; and the last moment arrived.

"Say good-by twice to me," said Hattie, the little invalid, rising up on her lounge to give him a farewell kiss.

"Why twice to you?" asked Frank.

"Because," she answered, with a sad, sweet smile, "if you do come home from the war, perhaps you won't find me here;" for the child had a notion that she was going to die.

"O sissy," exclaimed Frank, "don't say so; J shall come back, and I shall find you well."

"Yes," replied Hattie, sorry that she had said any thing to make him feel bad; "we will think so, dear brother." And she smiled again; just as angels smile, Frank thought.

"Besides, this isn't my good-by for good, you know," said he. "I shall get a furlough, and come home and see you all, before I leave for the seat of war with my regiment." Frank couldn't help feeling a sort of pride in speaking of *his regiment.* "And may-be you will all visit me in camp before I go."

"Come," called his father, at the door; "if we are going to catch this car, we must be off."

So Frank abbreviated his adieus, and ran.

"Wait, wait!" screamed Willie, pulling his cap on. "Me go, me go!"

"Go where, you little witch?" cried Helen.

"Me go to war, along with my bwother Fwank. Put down webellion," pouted the child, shouldering his gun, and trudging out of the door in eager haste, fearing lest he should be left behind.

Mrs. Manly was parting from her son on the doorstep, putting back a stray curl from his cheek, smoothing his collar, and whispering, with wet eyes and quivering lips, "My child, remember!"

"I will — good-by!" were Frank's last words; and he hastened after his father, just pausing on the next corner to look around at the faces in the door of his home, and wave his hat at them. There was Hattie, leaning on Helen's arm, and waving her handkerchief, which was scarcely whiter than that thin white face of hers; and there was his mother gazing after him with steadfast eyes of affection and blessing, while her hands were fully occupied in restraining that small but fiery patriot, Willie, who, with his cap over his eyes, was vehemently struggling to go with his bwother Fwank.

This was the tableau, the final picture of home, which remained imprinted on Frank's memory. For the corner was passed, and the doorway and windows of the dear old house, and the dearer faces there, were lost to sight. He would have delayed, in order to get one more look; but already the tinkling bells gave

warning of the near approach of the horse-car, and
he and his father had no more than time to reach the
Main Street, when it came up, and stopped to take
them in.

In but little more than an hour's time, by far the
most important step in Frank's life had been taken.
He had enlisted.

"Well," said his father, after Frank, with a firm
and steady hand, had written his name, "it is done
now. You are a brave boy!" — with a tear of pride,
as he regarded his handsome, spirited young volunteer,
and thought that not many fathers had such promising sons.

While they were at the recruiting office, one of
their neighbors came in.

"What!" he exclaimed, "you here? on business?"

"Patriotic business," replied Mr. Manly, showing
his son with a fond father's emotion. "He has vol-
unteered, neighbor Winch."

"And you give your consent?"

"I do, most certainly, since he feels it his duty to go,
and his mother is willing."

Neighbor Winch stood speechless for a moment,
the muscles of his mouth working. "I have just
heard," he said, in an agitated voice, "that my son
John has enlisted *without* my consent; and I have

come here to ascertain the fact. Do you know any thing about it, Frank?"

"I suppose I do," replied Frank, with some reluctance. "He enlisted three days ago. He wanted me to go with him then; but I —— "

"You what?" said neighbor Winch.

"I couldn't, without first getting permission from my father and mother," explained Frank.

"O, if my John had only acted as noble a part!" said the neighbor. "It's a bad beginning for a boy to run away. He has nearly broken his mother's heart."

"Well, well, neighbor," observed Mr. Manly, consolingly, "reflect that it's in a good cause. Jack might have done worse, you know."

"Yes, yes. He never was a steady boy, as you know. He has set out to learn three different trades, and got sick of them all. I couldn't keep him at school, neither. Of late nothing would do but he must be a soldier. If I thought he'd stick to it, and do his duty, I wouldn't say a word. But he'll get tired of carrying a gun, too, before he has seen hard service. Where is he? Do you know, Frank?"

"He is in camp, in the Jackson Blues," said Frank. "I am going as drummer in the same company."

"I'm glad of that," replied Mr. Winch. "For, though he is so much older than you, I think you always have had an influence over him, Frank — a good influence, too." And the neighbor took the young volunteer's hand.

Frank's eyes glistened — he felt so touched by this compliment, and so proud that his father had heard it, and could go home and tell it to his mother and sisters.

Neighbor Winch went on: "I want you to see John, as soon as you can, Frank, and talk with him, and try to make him feel how wrongly he has acted ——"

Here the poor man's voice failed him; and Frank, sympathizing with his sorrow, was filled with gratitude to think that he had never been tempted to grieve his parents in the same way.

Mr. Manly accompanied his son to the railroad depot, and saw him safely in the cars that were to convey him to camp, and then took leave of him. The young volunteer would have forgotten his manhood, and cried, if the eyes of strangers had not been upon him; even as it was, his voice broke when he said his last good-by, and sent back his love to his mother and sisters and little Willie.

III.

UNDER CANVAS.

THE cars were soon off; and the heart of Frank swelled within him as he felt himself now fairly embarked in his new adventure.

Soon enough the white tents of the camp rose in sight. The Stars and Stripes floating under the blue sky, the soldiers in their blue uniforms, the sentinels with their glittering bayoneted guns pacing up and down, and above all, the sound of a drum, which he considered now to be a part of his life, made him feel himself already a hero.

Several other recruits had come down in the train with him, accompanied by an officer. Frank was a stranger to them all. But he was not long without acquaintances, for he had scarcely alighted at the depot, when he saw coming towards him his neighbor and chum, Jack Winch, in soldier clothes — a good-looking young fellow, a head taller and some two years older than himself.

" Hello, Jack! how are you ? "

"Tip-top!" said Jack, looking happy as a prince.

The officer who had brought down the recruits went with them to the quartermaster's department, and gave orders for their outfit. When Frank's turn came, his measure was taken, and an astonishing quantity of army clothing issued to him. He had two pairs of drawers, two shirts, two pairs of stockings, a blouse, a dress coat, an overcoat, a cap, a pair of shoes, a pair of pantaloons, and a towel. Besides these he received a knapsack, with two blankets; a haversack, with a tin plate, knife and fork, and spoon; and a tin cup and canteen. He had also been told that he should get his drum and drumsticks; but in this he was disappointed. The department was out of drums.

"Never mind!" said Jack, consolingly. "You may consider yourself lucky to draw your clothes so soon. I had to wait for mine till I was examined and sworn in. The surgeons are so lazy, or have so much to do, or something, it may be a week before you'll be examined."

Frank was soon surrounded by acquaintances whom he scarcely recognized at first, they looked so changed and strange to him in their uniforms.

"How funny it seems," said he, "to be shaking hands with soldiers!"

"These are our tents," said Jack. "They all have their names, you see."

Which fact Frank had already noticed with no little astonishment.

The names were lettered on the canvas of the tents in characters far more grotesque than elegant. One was called the " Crystal Palace ; " another, the " Mammoth Cave ; " a third bore the mystical title of " Owl House ; " while a fourth displayed the sign of the " Arab's Home ; " &c.

" My traps are in the ' Young Volunteer,' " said Jack. " We give it that name, because we are all of us young fellows in there. You can tie up here too," — entering the tent, — " if you want to."

Frank gladly accepted the proposition. " How odd it must seem," he said, " to live and sleep under canvas ! "

" You'll like it tip-top, when you get used to it," remarked Jack, with an air of old experience.

Frank made haste to take off his civil suit and put on his soldier clothes. Jack pronounced the uniform a splendid fit, and declared that his friend looked " stunning."

" But you must have your hair cut, Frank. Look here ; this is the fighting trim ! " and Jack Winch, pulling off his cap, made Frank laugh till the tears came into his eyes, at the ludicrous sight. Jack's hair had been clipped so close to his head that it was no longer than mouse's hair, giving him a peculiarly grim and antique appearance.

"You look like Sindbad's Old Man of the Sea!" exclaimed Frank. "I won't have my hair cut that way!" — feeling of his own soft brown curls, which his mother was so fond of, and which he meant to preserve, if only for her sake.

"Pshaw! you look like a girl! Come, Frank, there's a fellow in the 'Owl House' that cuts all the hair for our company."

But here an end was put to the discussion by some of the boys without crying, "Dinner!"

"Dinner!" repeated Jack. "Hurrah! let's go and draw our rations."

Three or four young volunteers now came into the tent, and, opening their haversacks, drew forth their tin plates, knives and forks. Frank did the same, and observing that they all took their tin cups, he took his also, and followed them, with quite as much curiosity as appetite, to the cook-shop, where a large piece of bread and a thick slice of boiled beef was dealt out to each, together with a cup of coffee.

"How droll it seems to eat rations!" said Frank, on their return, seating himself on his bed, — a tick filled with straw, — and using his lap for a table.

The bread was sweet; but the beef was of not quite

so fine a quality as Frank had been used to at home; and the coffee was not exactly like his mother's.

"Here, have some milk," said Jack. "I've an account open with this woman"—a wrinkled old creature, who came into the tent with a little girl, bearing baskets of cake and fruits, and a can of milk.

"No, I thank you," said Frank. "I may as well begin with the fare I shall have to get used to some time, for I mean to send all my pay home to my folks except what I'm actually obliged to use myself."

"You'll be a goose if you do!" retorted Jack. "I shan't send home any of mine. I'm my own man now, ye see, and what I earn of Uncle Sam I'm going to have a gallus old time with, you may bet your life on that!"

Frank drew a long breath, for he felt that the time had now come to have the talk with his friend which Mr. Winch had requested.

"I saw your father, this morning, Jack."

"Did ye though? What did the old sinner have to say?"

"I don't like to hear you call your father such names," said Frank, seriously. "And if you had seen how bad he felt, when he spoke of your enlisting ——"

"Pshaw, now, Frank! don't be green! don't get into a pious strain, I beg of ye! You'll be the laughing-stock of all the boys, if ye do."

Frank blushed to the eyes, not knowing what reply to make. He had felt no little pride in Mr. Winch's responsible charge to him, and had intended to preach to his more reckless companion a good, sound, moral discourse on this occasion. But to have his overtures received in this manner was discouraging.

"Come," continued Jack, taking something from the straw, "we are soldiers now, and must do as soldiers do. Have a drink, Frank?" — presenting a small bottle.

"What is it?" Frank asked, and when told, "Brandy," he quickly withdrew the hand he had extended. "No, I thank you, Jack. I am not going to drink any thing of that sort, unless I need it as a medicine. And I am sorry to see you getting into such habits so soon."

"Habits? what habits?" retorted Jack, blushing in his turn. "A little liquor don't hurt a fellow. *I* take it only as a medicine. You musn't go to being squeamish down here, I tell you." And Jack drank a swallow or two, smacking his lips afterwards, as he returned the cork to the bottle.

By this time Frank's courage was up — his moral courage, I mean, which is more rare, as it is far more noble, than any merely physical bravery in the face of danger.

"I don't mean to be squeamish," he said; "but

right is right, and wrong is wrong, Jack. And what
was wrong for us at home isn't going to be right for
us here. I, for one, believe we can go through this
war without doing any thing that will make our
parents ashamed of us when we return."

"My eye!" jeered his companion; "and do you
fancy a little swallow of brandy is going to make my
folks ashamed of me?"

"It isn't the single swallow I object to, Jack; it's
the habit of drinking. That's a foolish thing, to say
the least, for young fellows, like you and me, to get
into; and we all know what it leads to. Who wants
to become a tobacco-spitting, rum-drinking, filthy old
man?"

"Ha, ha, ha," laughed Jack; rather feebly, however, for he could not help feeling that Frank was as
much in the right as he was in the wrong. "You
look a long ways ahead, it seems to me. I haven't
thought of being an old man yet."

"If we live, we shall be men, and old men, too,
some day," said Frank, without minding his sneers.
"And you know we are laying the foundations of our
future characters now."

"That's what your mother, or your Sunday school
teacher, has been saying to you."

"No matter who has said it. I know it's true, and I
hope I never shall forget it. I mean to become a true,

honest man if I live; and now, I believe, is the time to begin."

"O, no doubt you'll be great things," grinned Jack.

The tone in which he said this was highly offensive; and Frank was provoked to retort, —

"You don't seem even to have thought what you are going to be. You try first one thing, then another, and stick to nothing. That's what your father said this morning, with tears in his eyes."

Jack turned red as fire, either with anger or shame, or both, and seemed meditating a passionate reply, when some of his companions, who had been eating their rations outside, entered the tent.

"Come in, boys," cried Jack, "and hear Frank preach. You didn't know we had a chaplain in our company—did ye? That's the parson, there, with the girl's hair. He can reel you off sermons like any thing. Fire away, Frank, and show the boys."

"Yes, steam up, parson," said Joe Harris, "and give us a specimen."

"Play away, seven," cried Ned Ellis, as if Frank had been a fire-engine of that number.

These, together with other facetious remarks, made Frank so ashamed and confused that he could not say a word. For experience had not yet taught him that even the most reckless and depraved, however they may laugh at honest seriousness in a companion, cannot help respecting him for it in their hearts.

"You needn't blush so, young chap," said tall Abram Atwater, a stalwart, square-shouldered, square-featured young man of twenty, who alone had not joined in the derisive merriment. "It won't hurt any of these fellows to preach to them, and they know it."

Frank cast a grateful look at the tall soldier, who, though almost a stranger to him, had thus generously taken his part against some who professed to be his friends. He tried to speak, but could not articulate a word, he was still feeling so hurt by Jack's ingratitude. Perhaps his pride was as much wounded as his friendship; for, as we have hinted, he had been a good deal puffed up with the idea of his influence over Jack. This incident, as we shall see, had a bad effect upon Frank himself; for, instead of persevering in the good work he had undertaken, he was inclined to give up all hope of exerting an influence upon any body.

In the mean time Jack was washing down the sermon, as he said, with more brandy.

"'Twas such an awful dry discourse, boys;" and he passed the bottle around to the others, who all drank, except Abram Atwater. That stalwart young soldier stood in the midst of the tent, straight and tall, with his arms calmly folded under his blue cape (a favorite attitude of his), and merely shook his head, with a mild and tolerant smile, when the liquor was passed to him.

Such was the beginning of Frank's camp life. It was not long before he had recovered from his confusion, and was apparently on good terms with his messmates. He spent the afternoon in walking about the camp; watching some raw recruits at their drill; watching others playing cards, or checkers, or backgammon; getting acquainted, and learning the ways of the camp generally.

So the day passed; and that night Frank lay for the first time soldier-fashion, under canvas. He went to bed with his clothes on, and drew his blanket over him. It was not like going to bed in his nice little room at home, with Willie snuggled warmly beside him; yet there was a novelty in this rude and simple mode of life that was charming. His companions, who lay upon the ground around him, kept him awake with their stories long after the lights were out; but at length, weary with the day's excitement, he fell asleep.

There, — a dweller now in the picturesque white city of tents gleaming in the moonlight, ruggedly pillowed on his soldier's couch, those soft brown curls tossed over the arm beneath his head, — the drummer boy dreamed of home. The last night's consultation and the morning's farewells were lived over again in the visions of his brain; and once more his mother visited his bedside ; and again his father accompanied him to the recruiting office. But now the recruiting office was changed into a barber's shop, which seemed to be a tent supported by a striped pole; where, at John Winch's suggestion, he was to have his hair trimmed to the fighting-cut. The barber was a stiff-looking officer in epaulets, who heated a sword red-hot in an oven, while Frank preached to him a neat little sermon over his ration. Then the epaulets changed to a pair of roosters with flaming red combs, that flapped their wings and crowed. And the barber, approaching Frank with his red-hot sword, made him lie on his back to be shaved. Then followed an excruciating sense of having his hair pulled and his face scraped and burnt, which made him move and murmur in his sleep; until, a ruthless attempt being made to thrust the sword up his nostrils, he awoke.

Shouts of laughter greeted him. His companions had got up at midnight, lighted a candle, and burnt a cork, with which they had been giving him an artificial mustache and whiskers. He must have been a ludicrous sight, with his countenance thus ornamented, sitting up on his bed, rubbing his eyes open, and staring about him, while Winch and Harris shrieked with mirth, and Ned Ellis flapped his arms and crowed.

Frank put up his hand to his head. O grief! his

curls had been mangled by dull shears in the unskilful
hands of John Winch. The depredator was still brandishing the miserable instrument, which he had borrowed for the occasion of the fellow who cut the company's hair in the " Owl House."

Frank's sudden awaking, astonishment, and chagrin
were almost too much for him. He could have cried
to think of a friend playing him such a trick; and to
think of his lost curls! But he had made up his mind
to endure every thing that might befall him with
unflinching fortitude. He must not seem weak on an
occasion like this. His future standing with his comrades might depend upon what he should say and do
next. So he summoned all his stoutness of heart, and
accepted the joke as good-naturedly as was possible
under the circumstances.

" I wish you'd tell me what the fun is," he said, " so
that I can laugh too."

" Give him the looking-glass," cried Jack Winch,
holding the candle, while Ellis stopped crowing, to
bring a little three-cornered fragment of a broken
mirror, by which Frank was shown the artistic burnt-
cork work on his face. He could hardly help laughing
himself at his own hideousness, now that the first
disagreeable sense of being the sport of his friends had
passed.

" I hope you have had fun enough to pay for

waking me up out of the queerest dream any body ever had," he said. And he told all about the barber, and the epaulets that became roosters, and the red-hot sword for a razor, &c. Then, looking at himself again in the piece of glass, he called out, " Give me those shears;" and taking them, he manfully cut off his mutilated curls. " There, that isn't exactly the fighting-cut, Jack, but 'twill do. Now, boys, tell some more of those dull stories, and I guess I can go to sleep again."

And he lay down once more, declining to accept an urgent invitation to preach.

" There, boys," said stout Abram Atwater, who had sat all the time cross-legged, a silent, gravely-smiling spectator of the scene, " you shan't fool him any more. He has got pluck; he has shown it. And now let him alone."

IV.

THE OLD DRUMMER AND THE NEW DRUM.

As yet, Frank had no drum. Neither had he any scientific knowledge of the instrument. He was ambitious of entering upon his novel occupation, and was elated to learn, the next morning, that he was to begin his acquaintance with the noble art of drumming that very day.

"The sergeant is inquiring for you," said Abram Atwater, with his mild, pleasant smile, calling him out of the tent.

Frank, who was writing a letter to his mother, on his knapsack, jumped up with alacrity, hid his paper, and ran out to see what was wanted.

"This way, Manly," said the sergeant. "Here's the man that's to give you lessons. Go with him."

The teacher was a veteran drummer, with a twinkling gray eye, a long, thick, gray mustache, and a rather cynical way of showing his teeth under it. He had some drumsticks thrust into his pocket, but no drum.

(37)

"I suppose," thought Frank, "we shall find our drums in the woods;" into which his instructor straightway conducted him in order to be away from the diversions and noises of the camp.

Frank was disappointed. The veteran gave him his first exercise — on a board!

"I thought I was to learn on a drum," he ventured to suggest, looking up, not without awe, at the bushy mustache.

"You don't want a drum till you know how to drum," said the veteran.

"But I should think it would be better ——"

"Wait!" lifting his drumstick. "Do you understand what we are here for?"

"To learn to drum," replied Frank, in some astonishment.

"To learn to drum," repeated the veteran, a curious smile just raising the corners of that grizzled mustache. "You understand correctly. Now, am I your teacher, or are you mine?"

"You are mine, sir," answered the boy, still more amazed.

"Right again!" exclaimed the professor. "That's the way I understood it; but I might be wrong, you know. We are all liable to be wrong — are we not?"

"Yes, sir."

Frank stared.

" Good again! But now it is understood correctly; I am your instructor, and you are not mine; that is it."

Frank assented.

"Very well! Now listen. Since I am to give you lessons, and you are not to give me lessons, you will follow the method I propose, and excuse me if I decline to follow your method. That is reasonable, — isn't it?"

"Certainly, sir," murmured the abashed pupil.

"The point settled, then, we will proceed," said the veteran, with the same incomprehensible, half-sarcastic, half-humorous, but now quite good-natured smile lighting up his grim visage.

"But before we proceed," said Frank, "may I just say what I was going to?"

The old drummer lifted both his sticks, and his eyebrows too (not to speak of his shaggy mustache), in surprise at the lad's audacity.

"Do you want me to report you as insubordinate?" he asked, after a pause, during which the two regarded each other somewhat after the fashion of two dogs making acquaintance — a tall, leering old mastiff looking surlily down at the advances of an anxious yet stout and unflinching young spaniel.

. "No, sir," answered Frank. "But I thought ——"

"You thought! What business have you to think?"

"No business, perhaps," Frank admitted, confronting

the weather-beaten old drummer with his truthful, undaunted, fine young face. "But I can't help thinking, sir, for all that."

"You can help expressing your thoughts out of season, though," said the veteran.

"I will try to in future, sir," answered Frank, laughing.

At the same time a smile of genuine benevolence softened the tough, ancient visage of the veteran; and they proceeded with the lesson.

After it was over, the teacher said to the pupil,—

"Now, my young friend, I will hear that observation or question of yours, whatever it is."

"I think I have answered it for myself," said Frank. "I was going to say, I should think it would be better to learn to drum on a drum; but I see now, if I get to roll the sticks on a board, which is hard, I can roll them so much the better on a drumhead, which is elastic."

"Right, my young friend," replied the veteran, approvingly. "And in the mean time, we avoid a good deal of unpleasant noise, as you see." For he had other pupils practising under his eye in the woods, not far from Frank.

"And I should like to ask — if I could have permission," began Frank, archly.

"Ask me any thing you please, out of lesson-hours."

And the old drummer patted the young drummer's shoulder.

Frank felt encouraged. He was beginning to like his teacher, notwithstanding his odd ways; and he hoped the old man was beginning to like him.

"I want to know, then, if you think I will make a drummer?"

"And what if you will not?"

"Then I shall think I ought to give up the idea of it at once; for I don't want to be second-rate in any thing I once undertake."

"And you have been just a little discouraged over your first lesson? and would be willing now to give up?"

"No, sir. I should feel very bad to be obliged to give up the drum."

"Very well. Then I can say something to comfort you. Stick to it, as you have begun, and you will make a drummer."

"A first-rate one?" Frank asked, eagerly.

"First-rate, or else I am no judge."

"I am glad!" and the delighted pupil fairly jumped for joy.

From that time the two got on capitally together. Frank soon became accustomed to the veteran's eccentric manners, and made great proficiency in his exercises. And it was not long before the hard-featured

old drummer began to manifest, in his way, a great deal
of friendly interest in his young pupil.

"Now, my boy," said he one day, after Frank had
been practising successfully the "seven-stroke roll,"
greatly to the satisfaction of his instructor,— "now,
my boy, I think you can be safely intrusted with your
comrade."

"My comrade?" queried the pupil.

"I mean, your better half."

"My better half?"

Frank was mystified.

"Yes, your wife." And the grizzly mustache curled
with quiet humor.

"I must be a married man without knowing it!"
laughed Frank.

"Your ship, then," said the veteran, dryly. "Come
with me."

And conducting Frank to his tent, he took from one
side an object covered with a blanket.

"My ship!" cried Frank, joyfully, already guessing
what treasure was now to be his.

"Your sword, then, if you like that name better.
For what his sword is to a hero, what his ship is to a
true sailor, what a wife is to a true husband,— such, my
young friend, to a genuine drummer is his drum."

So saying, the veteran threw aside the covering, and
presented to his pupil the long-coveted prize. The

boy's eyes shone with pleasure, and (as he wrote that evening to his parents) he was so happy he could have hugged both the old drummer and the new drum.

"I selected it for you, and you may be sure it is a good one. It won't be any handsomer, but, if you use it well, it won't be really much the worse, for going through a campaign or two with you. For it is with drums as it is with the drummers; they grow old, and get some honorable scratches, and some unlucky bruises, and now and then a broken head; but, God prospering them, they come out, at last, ugly to look at, perhaps" (the veteran stroked his mustache), "but well-seasoned, and sound, and very truly at your service."

Frank thought he saw a tear in his twinkling gray eye, and he was so much affected by it, that he caught his hand in both of his, exclaiming, "Bless you, dear sir! Dear, good sir, God bless you!"

The old man winked away the moisture from his eye, smiling still, but with a quivering lip, and patted him gently on the shoulder, without saying a word.

Frank had the sense to perceive that the interview was now over; the veteran wished to be left alone; and, with the new drum at his side, he left the tent, proud and happy, and wishing in his heart that he could do something for that singular, kind old man.

As Frank was hastening to his tent, he was met by one of the captains in his regiment, who, see

ing the right beaming face and new drum, accosted
him.

"So, you are a drummer boy — are you?"

"Yes, sir, I am learning to be one," said Frank,
modestly.

Now, these two had seen each other often in camp,
and the captain had always regarded Frank with a
smile of interest and kindness, and Frank (as he wrote
home) had "always liked the looks of the captain first-
rate."

"I saw you, I think, the day you came here," said
the captain. "You had some curls then. What has
become of them?"

Frank's lip twitched, and he cast down his eyes,
ashamed to betray any lingering feeling on that subject.

"The boys cut them off in my sleep, sir."

"The rogues!" exclaimed the captain. "And what
did you do?"

Frank lifted his eyes with a smile. "I partly finished
them myself — they had haggled them so; and the
next day I found a man to cut my hair nicely."

"Well, it is better so, perhaps: short hair for a soldier. But I liked those curls. They reminded me of
a little sister of mine — she is gone now —," in a low,
mellow tone. "Are you attached to any company?"

"I am enlisted in the Jackson Blues."

"What is your name?"

"Frank Manly, sir."

"Are you any relation to Mrs. Manly, of —— ?"

"She is my mother, sir," said Frank, with proud affection.

"Is it possible! Mrs. Manly's son! Indeed, you look like her."

"Do you know my mother, sir?"

"My lad," said the captain, "I used to go to school to her. But, though I have heard of her often, I haven't seen her for years."

"I shall write to her, and tell her about you," said Frank, delighted. "She will be glad to hear that I have found so good a friend."

"Ask her," said the captain, "if she remembers Henry Edney, who used to go to school to her in ——. She will recollect me, I am sure. And give my very kind regards to her, and to your father; and tell them I regret I didn't see you before you enlisted, for I want just such a drummer boy in my company. But never mind," he added quickly, as if conscious of having spoken indiscreetly, "you will do your duty where you are, and I will try to do mine, for we must have only one thought now — to serve our country."

They separated, with more kind words on the captain's part, and with expressions of gratitude on the part of Frank, who felt that, to compensate him for

John Winch's treachery, he was already securing the friendship of a few of the best of men.

You may be sure the boy wrote to his mother all about the interview, and told her how sorry he was that he had not enlisted in Captain Edney's company; not only because he liked his new friend's kindness and affable manners so well, but also because there existed in the ranks of the Jackson Blues a strong prejudice against their own officers. Captain —— was almost a stranger to his men, and seemed determined to continue so. He seldom appeared amongst them, or showed any interest in their welfare. He had never once drilled them, but left that duty entirely to the sergeant. They consequently accused him boldly of laziness, ignorance, and conceit — three qualities which men always dislike in their superiors. How different was Captain Edney!

V.

FUN IN CAMP.

FRANK now practised his lessons on his drum, and was very happy. He had passed the surgical examination a few days after his arrival in camp, and been duly sworn into the service. This latter ceremony made a strong impression on his mind. He stood in the open air, together with a number of new recruits, and heard the Articles of War read; after which they all took off their caps, and held up their right hands, while the oath was administered.

One day, on returning to camp after his lesson in the woods, he was astonished to see Jack Winch, with his cap off, his fighting-cut displayed to all beholders, and his fist shaking, marched off by armed soldiers.

"What are they doing with Jack?" he hastened to inquire of Abram Atwater, who stood among his comrades with his arms composedly crossed under his cape.

"He is put under guard," said the tall, taciturn soldier. (47)

"You see," cried Joe Harris, coming up, "Jack had tipped the bottle once too often, and got noisy. The sergeant told him to keep still. 'Dry up yourself,' says Jack. 'Start,' says the sergeant; and he took hold of him to push him towards the tent; but the next he knew, he got a blow square in the face, — Jack was so mad!"

"Come, boys," said Ned Ellis, "le's go over and see how he likes the fun."

The proposal was accepted; and presently a strong deputation of the Blues went to pay a visit to their disgraced comrade. Arrived at the guard tent, a couple of sentinels crossed their bayonets before them. But although they could not enter, they could look in; and there, seated on the ground, they saw Jack, in a position which would have appeared excessively ludicrous to Frank, but that it seemed to him too piti- ful to behold any comrade so degraded. In conse- quence of his continued fury and violence, Jack had been secured in this fashion. Imagine a grotesque letter N, to which feet, arms, and a head have been added, and you have some idea of his posture, as seen in profile. His knees were elevated; forming the upper angle of the letter. The lower angle was rep- resented by that portion of the body which forms the seat of the human animal. The arms were passed over the upper angle, that is, the knees, and kept in their place by handcuffs on the wrists, and by a musket thrust through, over the arms and under the knees.

"Can't you untie them iron knots with your teeth, Jack?" said Joe, meaning the handcuffs.

"How do you like the back to your chair?" said Ned.

"Let's see ye turn a somerset backwards, Jack."

And so forth. But Frank did not insult him in his disgrace.

Winch was by this time sufficiently sobered and humbled. He destroyed the symmetry of the N by doubling himself ingloriously over his knees and hiding his face between them.

"Got the colic, Jack?" asked Harris — "you double up so."

Winch glared up at him a moment, — a ludicrous picture, with that writhing face and that curious fighting-cut, — but cast down his eyes again, sulkily, and said nothing.

"Come away, boys," whispered Frank. "Don't stay here, making fun of him. Why do you?"

"Jack," said Ellis, "we're going to take a drink. Won't you come along with us?" — tauntingly.

And the Blues dispersed, leaving poor Jack to his own bitter reflections.

He had learned one thing — who his friends were.

4

On being released, he shunned Harris and Ellis especially, for a day or two, and paid his court to Frank.

"I'm going to tell you something, Frank," said he, as they were once at the pond-side, washing their plates after dinner. "I'm going to leave the company."

"Leave the Blues?" said Frank.

"Yes, and quit the service. I've got sick of it."

"But I thought you liked it so well."

"Well, I did at first. It was a kind of novelty. Come, le's leave it. I will."

"But how can you?"

"Easy enough. I am under age, and my father 'll get me off."

"I should think you would be ashamed to ask him to," Frank could not help saying, with honest contempt.

Jack was not offended this time by his plainness, for he had learned that those are not, by any means, our worst friends, who truly tell us our faults.

"I don't care," he said, putting on an air of recklessness. "I ain't going to lead this miserable dog's life in camp any longer, if I have to desert" — lowering his voice to a whisper; "we can desert just as easy as not, Frank, if we take a notion."

"I, for one," said Frank, indignantly, "shan't take a

notion to do any thing so dishonorable. We enlisted of our own free will, and I think it would be the meanest and most dishonest thing we could do to —— "

" Hush ! " whispered Jack. " There's Atwater; he'll hear us."

At midnight the drummer boy was awakened by a commotion in the tent.

" Come, Frank," said some one, pulling him violently, " we are going to have some great fun. Hurrah ! "

Frank jumped up. The boys were leaving the tent. He had already suspected that mischief was meditated, and, anxious to see what it was, he ran out after them.

He found the company assembled in a dark, mysterious mass in the street before the row of tents.

" Get a rope around his neck," said one.

" Burn the tent," said another.

" With him in it," said a third.

" What does it all mean ? " Frank inquired of his friend Atwater, whom he found quietly listening to the conspirators.

" A little fun with the Gosling, I believe," said Atwater, with a shrug. " They'd better let him alone."

"The Gosling" was the nickname which the Blues had bestowed on their captain.

After a hurried consultation among the ringleaders, the company marched to the tent where the Gosling slept. Only Atwater, Frank, and a few others lingered in the rear.

"I hope they won't hurt him," said Frank. "Ought we not to give the alarm?"

"And get the lasting ill-will of the boys?" said Atwater. "We can't afford that."-

The captain's tent was surrounded. Knives were drawn. Then, at a concerted signal, the ropes supporting the tent were cut. At the same time the captain's bed, which made a convenient protuberance in the side of the tent, was seized and tipped over, while tent-pole, canvas, and all, came down upon him in a mass.

"Help! guard! help!" he shrieked, struggling under the heap.

At the instant a large pile of straw, belonging to the quartermaster's department close by, burst forth in a sheet of flame which illumined the camp with its glare.

The boys now ran to their tents, laughing at the plight of the captain, as he issued, furious, from the ruins. Frank began to run too; but thinking that this would be considered an indication of guilt, he stopped. Atwater was at his side.

"We are caught," said Atwater, coolly. "There's the guard." And he folded his arms under his cape and waited.

"What shall we do?" said Frank, in great distress; not that he feared the advancing bayonets, but he remembered John Winch's arrest, and dreaded a similar degradation.

"There are two of them," said the half-dressed captain, pointing out Frank and his friend to the officer of the guard.

In his excitement he would have had them hurried off at once to the guard-tent. But fortunately the colonel of the regiment, who had been writing late in his tent, heard the alarm, and was already on the spot. He regarded the prisoners by the light of the burning straw. Frank, recovering from the trepidation of finding himself for the first time surrounded by a guard, and subject to a serious accusation, returned his look with a face beaming with courage and innocence. The colonel smiled.

"Have you been meddling with Captain ——'s bed, and cutting his tent down?" he asked.

"No, sir," said Frank, with a mien which bore witness to the truth.

"Do you know who set that fire?"

"No, sir."

"What are you out of your tent for?"

"I came to see the fun, sir. If it was wrong I am very sorry."

" What fun ? "

" The boys were going to have some fun; I didn't know what, and I came to see."

" What boys ? "

" All the boys in our company."

" Which of them did the things your captain complains of? "

"I don't know, sir. They were all together; and who tipped the bed, or cut the ropes, or set the fire, I can't tell."

" It seems they were all concerned, then."

" No, sir, not all. Some did the mischief, and the rest looked on."

" Did this person with you do any of the mischief? "

" No, sir; he was with me all the time, and we kept out of it."

" How happens it, then, that only you two are caught ? "

" All the rest ran."

" And why didn't you run ? "

" We had not been doing any thing to run for," said Frank, with convincing sincerity.

Atwater was then questioned, and gave similar answers.

"Captain ——," said the colonel, "I think it is evident these are not the persons who are most deserving of punishment. This boy, certainly, could not have been very deeply concerned in the assault, and I am inclined to place entire confidence in his story."

The captain himself appeared not a little ashamed of having accused one so young and ingenuous as the drummer boy. The prisoners were accordingly released, and the investigation of the affair was postponed until the morrow. Returning with Atwater to their tent, Frank could not repress the joy he felt at their fortunate escape. But Atwater took the whole affair with astonishing coolness, exhibiting no more emotion at their release than he had betrayed at their entrapment.

"What a fellow you are!" said Frank, staying his enthusiastic step, while his companion, with slow and stately pace, came up with him. "You don't seem to care for any thing."

"Those that care the most don't always show it," said Atwater, laconically, as they crept back into the tent.

All was hushed and dark within; but soon they heard whispers.

"Abe! Frank! that you?"

And they soon found that the tent was full of the fugitives, awaiting their return.

"What made you let 'em catch you? How did you get off?" were the first eager inquiries.

Dark as it was, Frank thought he could see Atwater shrug his shoulders and look to him for the required explanation. For Abram was a fellow of few words, and Frank was glib of speech.

So Frank, seated on his bed, related their adventure, to the great delight of the boys, who bestowed the warmest praises upon them for their spirit and fidelity. They had stood their ground when deserted by their companions; and, although they had told the truth about the whole company, they had not inculpated individuals. Thus Frank, as he afterwards learned with pleasure, had by his courage and truthfulness won both the confidence of his officers and the good will of his comrades.

The next day the company was called to an account for the offence. In reply to the captain's charges, the sergeant, acting as spokesman for the rest, stated the grievances of the men. The result was, that the captain received directions to exercise his company in the colonel's presence; and, complying reluctantly, demonstrated his own inefficiency in a manner which elicited the merriment of spectators, and even provoked the colonel to smile.

Soon after, in order to get rid of so incompetent an officer, and at the same time punish the insubordination of the men, it was resolved to disband the company. Thus was afforded to Frank the opportunity, which seemed to him almost providential, of joining Captain Edney's company, and to John Winch the desired chance to quit the service, of which he had so soon grown weary.

At this time the boys' fathers came down together to visit them. John had written home a pitiful letter, and Mr. Winch went to see about getting him off.

But Jack was no sooner out of the service than he wished to be in again. Frank, Atwater, and several others, had joined Captain Edney's company, and he determined to follow their example.

"O John!" groaned Mr. Winch, in despair at this inconstancy, "when will you learn to be a little more steady-minded? Here I have come expressly to plead your cause, and get you off; but before I have a chance, you change your mind again, and now nothing can persuade you to go home."

"Well," said John, "I didn't like the company I was in. I'm satisfied now, and I'm going to serve my country."

"Well, well," said Mr. Winch, "I shall let you do as you please. But reflect; you enlist with my consent now, and you must dismiss all hope of getting off next time you are sick of your bargain."

"O, I shan't be sick of it again," said John, as full

of ambition as he had lately been of discontent and disloyalty.

In the mean time Frank made the most of his father's visit. He showed him his new tent, his knapsack and accoutrements, and his handsome drum. He introduced him to the old drummer, and to Atwater, and to Captain Edney. The latter invited them both into his tent, and was so kind to them that Frank almost shed tears of gratitude, to think that his father could go home and tell what a favorite he was with his captain. Then, when dinner-time came, Frank drew a ration for his father, in order that he might know just what sort of fare the soldiers had, and how they ate it. And so the day passed. And Frank accompanied his father to the cars, and saw him off, sending a thousand good wishes home, and promising that he would certainly get a furlough the coming week, and visit them.

VI.

BREAKING CAMP.

FRANK was disappointed in not being able to keep that promise. An order came for the regiment to be ready to march in two days; in the mean time no furloughs could be granted.

"I am sorry for you, Frank," said Captain Edney; "and I would make an exception in your case, if possible."

"No, I don't ask that, sir," said Frank, stoutly. "I did want to see my folks again, but ——" He turned away his face.

"Well," said the captain, "I think it can be arranged so that you shall see them again, if only for a short time. You can warn them in season of our breaking camp, and they will meet you as we pass through Boston."

This was some consolation; although it was hard for Frank to give up the long-anticipated pleasure of visiting his family, and the satisfaction of relating his experience of a soldier's life to his sisters and mates.

(59)

He had thought a good deal, with innocent vanity, of the wonder and admiration he would excite, in his uniform, fresh from camp, and bound for the battle-fields of his country; but he had thought a great deal more of the happiness of breathing again the atmosphere of love and sympathy which we find nowhere but at home.

The excitement which filled the camp helped him forget his disappointment. The regiment was in fine spirits. It was impatient to be on the march. Its destination was not known; some said it was to be moved directly to Washington; others, that it was to rendezvous at Annapolis, and form a part of some formidable expedition about to be launched against the rebellion; but all agreed that what every soldier ardently desired was now before them — active service, and an enemy to be conquered.

The two days in which time the regiment was to prepare to move, became three days — four days — a week; unavoidable obstacles still delayed its departure, to the infinite vexation of Frank, who saw what a long furlough he might have enjoyed, and who repeatedly sent to his friends directions when and where to meet him, which he found himself obliged, each time, to write in haste and countermand the next morning. Such are some of the annoyances of a soldier's life.

But at length the long-delayed orders came. They were received with tumultuous joy by the impatient troops. It was necessary to send the ponderous baggage train forward a day in advance, and the tents were struck at once. All was bustle, animation, and hilarity in the camp; and a night of jubilee followed.

The drummer boy never forgot that night, amid all his subsequent adventures. While his companions were singing, shouting, and kindling fires, he could not help thinking, as he watched their animated figures lighted up by the flames, that this was, probably, the last night many of them would ever pass in their native state; that many would fall in battle, and find their graves in a southern soil; and that, perhaps, he himself was one of those who would never return.

"What are you thinking about, my bold soldier boy?" said a familiar voice, while a gentle hand slapped him on the back.

He turned and saw the bushy mustache of his friend and master, the old drummer, peering over his shoulder.

"O Mr. Sinjin!" said Frank. (The veteran wrote his name *St. John*, but every body called him *Sinjin*.) "I was afraid I should not see you again."

"Eh, and why not?"

"Because we are off in the morning, you know, and I couldn't find you to-day; and ——"

"And what, my lad?" said the old man, regarding him with a very tender smile.

"I couldn't bear the thought of going without seeing you once more."

"And what should a young fellow like you want to see an ugly, battered, miserable old hulk like me, for?"

"You have been very kind to me," said Frank, getting hold of the old man's hard, rough hand; "and I shall be sorry to part with you, sir, very sorry."

"Well, well." The veteran tried in vain to appear careless and cynical, as he commonly did to other people. "You are young yet. You believe in friendship, do you?"

"And don't you?" Frank earnestly inquired.

"I did once. A great while ago. But never mind about that. I believe in _you_, my boy. You have not seen the world and grown corrupted; you are still capable of a disinterested attachment; and may it be long before the thoughtlessness of some, and the treachery of others, and the selfishness of all, convince you that there is no such thing as a true friend." And the old drummer gave his mustache a fierce jerk, as if he had some grudge against it.

"O Mr. Sinjin," said Frank, "I shall never think so; and I am sure you do not. Haven't you any friends? Don't you really care for any body? Here are all

these boys; you know a good many of us, and every
body that knows you half as well as I do, likes you;
and we are going off now in a few hours, and some of
us will never come back; and don't you care?"

"Few, I fancy, think of me as you do," said the old
man, in a slightly choking voice. "They call me *Old
Sinjin*, without very much respect," grinning grimly
under his mustache.

"But they don't mean any thing by that; they
like you all the time, sir," Frank assured him.

"Well, like me or not," said the veteran, his smile
softening as he looked down at the boy's face upturned
so earnestly to his in the fire-light, "I have determined, if only for your sake, to share the fortunes of
the regiment."

"You have? O, good! And go with us?" cried
Frank, ready to dance for joy.

"I've got tired, like the rest of you, of this dull
camp life," said the old drummer; "and seeing you
pack your knapsack has stirred a little youthful blood
in my veins which I didn't suppose was there. I'm
off for the war with the rest of you, my boy;" and
he poked a coal from the fire to light his cigar, hiding
his face from Frank at the same time.

Frank, who could not help thinking that it was
partly for his sake that the old man had come to this
decision, was both rejoiced and sobered by this evi-

dence of friendship in one who pretended not to believe there was such a thing as true friendship in the world.

"I am so glad you are going; but I am afraid you are too old; and if any thing should happen to you——" Frank somehow felt that, in that case, he would be to blame.

The old man said nothing, but kept poking at the coal with a trembling hand.

"Here, Old Sinjin," said Jack Winch, "have a match. Don't be *singin'* your mustaches over the fire for nothing;" with an irreverent pun on the old man's name.

"Mr. Sinjin is going with us, Jack," said Frank.

"Is he? Bully for you, old chap!" said Jack, as the veteran, with a somewhat contemptuous smile, accepted the proffered match, and smoked away in silence. "We are going to have a gallus old time; nothing could hire me to stay at home." For Jack, when inspired by the idea of change, was always enthusiastic; he was then always going to have a gallus old time, if any body knows what that is. "Here goes my shoes," pitching those which he had worn from home into the fire.

"Why, Jack," said Frank, "what do you burn them for? Those were good shoes yet."

"I know it. But I couldn't carry them. The other

boys are burning up all their old boots and shoes. Uncle Sam furnishes us shoes now."

"But you should have sent them home, Jack; I sent mine along with my clothes. If you don't ever want them again yourself, somebody else may."

"What do I care for somebody else? I care more for seeing the old things curl and fry in the fire as if they was mad. O, ain't that a splendid blaze! It's light as day all over the camp. By jimmy, the fellows there are going to have a dance."

John ran off. Old Sinjin had also taken his departure, evidently not liking young Winch's company. Frank was left once more to his own thoughts, watching the picturesque groups about the fires. It was now midnight. The last of the old straw from the emptied ticks had been cast into the flames, and the broken tent-floors were burning brilliantly. Some of the wiser ones were bent on getting a little sleep. Frank saw Atwater spreading his rubber blanket on the ground, and resolved to follow his example. Others did the same; and with their woollen blankets over them, their knapsacks under their heads, and their feet to the fire, they bivouacked merrily under the lurid sky.

It was Frank's first experience of a night in the open air. The weather was mild, although it was now November; the fires kept them warm; and but for the noises made by the wilder sort of fellows they would have slept well in that novel fashion. The drummer boy sank several times into a light slumber, but as often started up, to hear the singing and laughter, and to see Atwater sleeping all the while calmly at his side, the wakeful ones making sport and keeping up the fires, and the flames glittering dimly on the stacks of arms. The last time he awoke it was day; and the short-lived camp-fires were paling their sad rays before the eternal glory of the sunrise.

The veteran Sinjin beat the drummers' call. Frank seized his drum and hurried to join his friend, — beating with him the last reveille which was to rouse up the regiment in the Old Bay State.

After roll-call, breakfast; then the troops were drawn up under arms, preparatory to their departure. A long train of a dozen cars was at the depot, in readiness to receive the regiment, which now marched out of the old camping-ground to the gay music of a band from a neighboring city.

After waiting an hour on the train, they heard the welcome whistle of the engine, and the still more welcome clang of the starting cars, and off they went amid loud cheers and silent tears.

Frank had no relatives or near friends in the crowd left behind, as many of his comrades had, but his heart beat fast with the thought that there were loved ones whom he should meet soon.

But the regiment reached Boston, and marched through the streets, and paraded on the Common; and all the while his longing eyes looked in vain for his friends, who never appeared. It seemed to him that nearly every other fellow in his company saw friends either on the march or at the halt, while he alone was left unnoticed and uncomforted. And so his anticipated hour of enjoyment was changed to one of bitterness.

Why was it? His last letter must have had time to reach his family. Besides, they might have seen by the newspapers that the regiment was coming. Why then did they fail to meet him? His heart swelled with grief as he thought of it, — he was there, so near home, for perhaps the last time, and nobody that he loved was with him during those precious, wasting moments.

But, suddenly, as he was casting his eyes for the twentieth time along the lines of spectators, searching for some familiar face, he heard a voice — not father's, or mother's, or sister's, but one scarcely less dear than the dearest.

"My bwother Fwank! me want my bwother Fwank!"

And turning, he saw little Willie running towards him, almost between the legs of the policemen stationed to keep back the crowd.

VII.

THROUGH BOSTON.

IF ever "bwother Fwank" felt a thrill of joy, it was then. Willie ran straight to his arms, in spite of the long-legged officer striding to catch him, and pulling down his neck, hugged him, and kissed him, and hugged and kissed him again, with such ardor that the delighted bystanders cheered, and the pursuing policeman stepped back with a laugh of melting human kindness.

"He's too much for me, that little midgit is," he said, returning to his place. "Does he belong to you, ma'am?" addressing a lady whose humid eyes betrayed something more than a stranger's interest in the scene.

"They are my children," said the lady. "Will you be so good, sir, as to tell the drummer boy to step this way?"

But already Frank was coming. How thankful he then felt that he was not a private, confined to the ranks! In a minute his mother's arm was about him,

(68)

and her kiss was on his cheek, and Helen was squeezing one hand, and his father the other, while Willie was playing with his drumsticks.

"I am all the more glad," he said, his face shining with gratitude and pleasure, "because I was just giving you up — thinking you wouldn't come at all."

"Only think," said Helen, "because you wrote on your letter, *In haste*, the postmaster gave it to Maggie Simpson yesterday to deliver, for she was going right by our house ; but Dan Alford came along and asked her to ride, and she forgot all about the letter, and would never have thought of it again, I suppose, if I hadn't seen the postmaster and set off on the track of it this morning. She had gone over to her aunt's, and I had to follow her there ; and then she had to go home again, to get the letter out of her other dress pocket ; but her sister Jane had by this time got on the dress, in place of her own, which was being washed, and worn it to school ; and so we had to go on a wild-goose chase after Jane."

"Well, I hope you had trouble enough for one letter ! " said Frank.

"But you haven't heard all yet," said Helen, laughing, "for when we found Jane, she had not the letter ; she had taken it out of the pocket, when she put the dress on, and left it on the bureau at home. So off again we started, Maggie and I, but before we got to her house, the letter had gone again — her mother had found it in the mean time, and sent it to us by the butcher boy. Well, I ran home, but no butcher boy had made his appearance; and, do you think, when I got to the meat shop, I found him deliberately sawing off a bone for his dog, with your letter in his greasy pocket."

"He had forgotten it too!" said Frank.

"Not he! but he didn't think it of very much importance, and he intended to bring it to us some time during the day — after he had fed his dog! By this time father had got news that the regiment was in town; and such a rush as we made for the horse-cars you never did see!"

"But Hattie! where is she?" Frank asked, anxiously.

Helen's vivacious face saddened a little.

"O, we came away in such a hurry we couldn't bring her, even if she had been well enough."

"Is she worse?"

"She gets no better," said Mrs. Manly, "and she herself thought she ought not to try to come. Maggie Simpson offered to stay with her."

"I am so sorry! I wanted to see *her*. Did she send any message to me?"

"Yes," said his mother. "She said, 'Give my love

to dear brother, and tell him to think of me sometimes.'"

"Think of her sometimes!" said Frank. "Tell her I shall always think of her and love her."

By this time Captain Edney, seeing Frank with his friends, came towards them. Frank hastened to hide his emotion; and, saluting the officer respectfully, said to him, with a glow of pleasure : —

"Captain Edney, this is my mother."

Captain Edney lifted his cap, with a bright smile.

"Well," he said, "this is a meeting I rather think neither of us ever looked forward to, when we used to spend those long summer days in the old school-house, which I hope you remember."

"I remember it well — and one bright-faced boy in particular," said Mrs. Manly, pressing his hand cordially.

"A rather mischievous boy, I am afraid I was; a little rebel myself, in those days," said the captain.

"Yet a boy that I always hoped much good of," said Mrs. Manly. "I cannot tell you how gratified I am to feel that my son is entrusted in your hands."

"You may be sure I will do what I can for him," said the captain, "if only to repay your early care of me."

He then conversed a few moments with Mr. Manly,

who was always well satisfied to stand a little in the background, and let his wife have her say first.

"And this, I suppose, is Frank's sister," turning to Helen. "I should have known her, I think, for she looks so much as you used to, Mrs. Manly, that I can almost fancy myself stepping up to her with my slate, and saying, 'Please, ma'am, show me about this sum?'"

Frank, in the mean time, was occupied in exhibiting to Willie his drum, and in preventing him, partly by moral suasion, but chiefly by main force, from gratifying his ardent desire to pound upon it.

"And here is our little brother," said the captain, lifting Willie, notwithstanding his struggles and kicks, and kissing his shy, pouting cheeks. "He'll make a nice drummer boy too, one of these days."

This royal flattery won the child over to his new friend immediately.

"Me go to war with my bwother Fwank! dwum, and scare webels!" panting earnestly over his important little story, which the captain was obliged to cut short.

"Well, Frank, I suppose you would like to spend the rest of the time with your friends. Be at the Old Colony depot at five o'clock. Meanwhile," — touching his cap, — "a pleasant time to all of you."

So saying, he left them, and Frank departed with

his friends, carrying his drum with him, to the great delight of little Willie, whose heart would have been broken if all hope of being allowed to drum upon it had been cut off by leaving it behind.

"Mrs. Gillett has invited us to bring you to her house," said Mrs. Manly. "I want to have a long talk with you there; and I want Mrs. Gillett's brother, the minister, to see you."

Frank was not passionately fond of ministers; and immediately an unpleasant image rose in his mind, of a solemn, black-coated individual, who took a mournful satisfaction in damping the spirits of young people by his long and serious conversations.

"You needn't strut so, Frank, if you *have* got soldier clothes on," laughed Helen. "I'll tell folks you are smart, if you are so particular to have them know it."

"Do, if you please," said Frank. "And I'll tell 'em you're handsome, if you'll put your veil down so they won't know but that I am telling the truth."

"There, Helen," said Mrs. Manly, "you've got your joke back with interest. Now I'd hold my tongue, if I was you."

"Frank and I wouldn't know each other if we didn't have a little fun together," said Helen. "Besides, we'll all feel serious enough by and by, I guess." For she loved her brother devotedly, much as she delighted to tease him; and she would have been glad to

drown in merry jests the thought of the final parting,
which was now so near at hand.

They were cordially received at Mrs. Gillett's house;
and there Mrs. Manly enjoyed the wished-for opportunity of talking with her son, and Willie had a chance
to beat the drum in the attic, and Mrs. Gillett secretly
emptied Frank's haversack of its rations of pork and
hard tack, and filled it again with excellent bread and
butter, slices of cold lamb, and sponge cake. Moreover, a delightful repast was prepared for the visitors,
at which Frank laughed at his own awkwardness, declaring that he had eaten from a tin plate so long, with
his drumhead for a table, that he had almost forgotten
the use of china and napkins.

"If Hattie was only here now!" he said, again and
again. For it needed only his invalid sister's presence,
during these few hours, to make him perfectly happy.

"Eat generously," said the minister, "for it may be
long before you sit at a table again."

"Perhaps I never shall," thought Frank, but he did
not say so lest he might hurt his mother's feelings.

The minister was not at all such a person as he had
expected to see, but only a very pleasant gentleman,
not at all stiffened with the idea that he had the dig-
nity of a profession to sustain. He was natural, friendly, and quite free from that solemn affectation which
now and then becomes second nature in ministers

some of us know, but which never fails to repel the sympathies of the young.

Mr. Egglestone was expecting soon to go out on a mission to the troops, and it was for this reason Mrs. Manly wished them to become acquainted.

"I wish you were going with our regiment," said Frank. "We have got a chaplain, I believe, but I have never seen him yet, or seen any body who has seen him."

"Well, I hope at least I shall meet you, if we both reach the seat of war," said the minister, drawing him aside. "But whether I do or not, I am sure that, with such a good mother as you have, and such dear sisters as you leave behind, you will never need a chaplain to remind you that you have something to preserve more precious than this mortal life of ours, — the purity and rectitude of your heart."

This was spoken so sincerely and affectionately that Frank felt those few words sink deeper into his soul than the most labored sermon could have done. Mr. Egglestone said no more, but putting his arm confidingly over the boy's shoulder, led him back to his mother.

And now the hour of parting had come. Frank's friends, including the minister, went with him to the cars. Arrived at the depot, they found it thronged with soldiers, and surrounded by crowds of citizens.

"O, mother!" said Frank, "you *must* see our drum-major, old Mr. Sinjin — my teacher, you know. There he is; I'll run and fetch him!"

He returned immediately, dragging after him the grizzled veteran, who seemed reluctant, and looked unusually stern.

"It's my mother and father, you know," said Frank. "They want to shake hands with you."

"What do they care for me?" said the old man, frowning.

Frank persisted, and introduced his father. The veteran returned Mr. Manly's salute with rigid military courtesy, without relaxing a muscle of his austere countenance.

"And this is my mother," said Frank.

With still more formal and lofty politeness, the old man bent his martial figure, and quite raised his cap from his old gray head.

"Madam, your very humble servant!"

"Mr. St. John!" exclaimed Mrs. Manly, in astonishment. "Is it possible that this is my old friend St. John?"

"Madam," said the veteran, with difficulty keeping up his cold, formal exterior, "I hardly expected you would do me the honor to remember one so unworthy;" bending lower than before, and raising his hat

again, while his lips twitched nervously under his thick
mustache.

"Why, where did you ever see him, mother?" cried
Frank, with eager interest.

"Mr. St. John was an old friend of your grandfather's,
Frank. Surely, sir, you have not forgotten the little
girl you used to take on your knee and feed with
candy?"— for the old man was still looking severe and
distant.

"I have not forgotten many pleasant things — and
some not so pleasant, which I would have forgotten by
every body." And the old drummer gave his mustache a vindictive pull.

"Be sure," said Mrs. Manly, "I remember nothing of
you that was not kind and honorable. I think you
must have known who my son was, you have been so
good to him. But why did you not inform him, or me
through him, who *you* were? I would have been so
glad to know about you."

"I hardly imagined that."— The old cynical smile
curled the heavy mustache. — "And if I could be of
any service to your son, it was needless for you to
know of it. I was Mr. St. John when you knew me;
but I am nobody but Old Sinjin now. Madam, I
wish you a very good-day, and much happiness.
Your servant, sir!"

And shaking hands stiffly, first with Mrs. Manly,

then with her husband, the strange old man stalked
away.

"Who is he? what is it about him?" asked Frank,
stung with curiosity. "Never did *I* think *you* knew
Old Sinjin."

"Your father knows about him, and I will tell *you*
some time," said Mrs. Manly, her eyes following the
retreating figure with looks of deep compassion. "In
the mean time, be very kind to him, very gentle and
respectful, my son."

"I will," said Frank, "but it is all so strange! I
can't understand it."

"Well, never mind now. Here is Captain Edney
talking with Helen and Mr. Egglestone, and Willie
is playing with his scabbard. Pretty well acquainted this young gentleman is getting!" said
Mrs. Manly, hastening to take the child away from
the sword.

"Pitty thord! pitty man!" lisped Willie, who had
fallen violently in love with the captain and his accoutrements. "Me and Helen, we like pitty man! We
go with pitty man!"

Helen blushed; while the captain, laughing, took a
piece of money from his pocket and gave it to Willie
for the compliment.

Frank, who had been absent a moment, now joined
the group, evidently much pleased at something.

"The funniest thing has happened! A fellow in our company, — and one of the best fellows he is too! but I can't help laughing! — he met his girl to-day, and they suddenly took it into their heads to get married; so they sent two of their friends to get their licenses for them, one, one way, and the other another way, for they live in different places. And the fellow's license has come, and the girl's hasn't, and they wouldn't have time to go to a minister's now if it had. It is too bad! but isn't it funny? The fellow is one of my very best friends. I wrote to you about him; Abe Atwater. There he is, with his girl!"

And Frank pointed out the tall young soldier, standing stately and taciturn, but with a strong emotion in that usually mild, grave face of his, perceptible enough to those who knew him. His girl was at his side, crying.

"How I pity her!" said Helen. "But he takes it coolly enough, I should think."

"He takes every thing that way," said Frank; "but you can't tell much by his face how he feels, though I can see he is biting hard to keep his heart down now, straight as he stands."

"I'll speak to her," said Helen; and while Frank accosted Atwater, she made acquaintance with the girl.

"Yes," said the soldier, "it would be better to know

I was leaving a wife behind, to think of me and look for my coming back. But I never knew she cared so much for me; and now it's too late."

"To think," said the girl to Helen, "he has loved me all along, but never told me, because he thought I wouldn't have him! And now he is going, and may be I shall never see him again! And we want to be married, and my license hasn't come!" And she poured out her sorrows into the bosom of the sympathizing Helen, with whom suffering and sympathy made her at once acquainted.   •

Just then the signal sounded for the train to be in readiness to start. And there were hurried partings, and tears in many a soldier's eye. And Frank's mother breathed into his ear her good-by counsel and blessing. And Atwater was bidding his girl farewell, when a man came bounding along the platform with a paper in his hand — the marriage license.

"Too late now!" said Atwater, with a glistening smile. "We are off!"

"But here is a minister!" cried Helen, — "Mr. Egglestone! — O, Captain Edney! have the train wait until this couple can be married. It won't take a minute!"

The case of the lovers was by this time well understood, not only by Captain Edney and Mr. Egglestone, but also by the conductor of the train and scores of soldiers and citizens. An interested throng crowded to witness the ceremony. The licenses were in the hands of the minister, and with his musket at *order arms* by his right side, and his girl at his left, Atwater stood up to be married, as erect and attentive as if he had been going through the company drill. And in a few words Mr. Egglestone married them; Frank holding Atwater's musket while he joined hands with his bride.

In the midst of the laughter and applause which followed, the soldier, with unchanging features, fumbled in his pocket for the marriage fee. He gave it to Mr. Egglestone, who politely handed it to the bride. But she returned it to her husband.

"You will need it more than I shall, Abram!" — forcing it, in spite of him, back into his pocket. "Good-by!" she sobbed, kissing him. "Good-by, my husband!"

This pleasing incident had served to lighten the pain of Frank's parting with his friends. When sorrowful farewells are to be said, no matter how quickly they are over. And they were over now; and Frank was on the departing train, waving his cap for the last time to the friends he could not see for the tears that dimmed his eyes.

And the cars rolled slowly away, amid cheers which drowned the sound of weeping. And the bride who

had had her husband for a moment only, and lost him,
— perhaps forever, — and the mother who had given
her son to her country, — perhaps never to receive
him back, — and other wives, and mothers, and fathers, and sisters, were left behind, with all the untold
pangs of grief and anxious love in their hearts, gazing
after the long swift train that bore their loved ones
away to the war.

VIII.

ANNAPOLIS.

AND the train sped on; and the daylight faded fast; and darkness shut down upon the world. And still the train sped on.

When it was too dark to see any thing out of the car windows, and Frank was tired of the loud talking around him, he thought he would amuse himself by nibbling a little " hard tack." So he opened his haversack, and discovered the cake, and bread and butter, and cold lamb, with which some one who loved him had stored it. He was so moved by this evidence of thoughtful kindness that it was some time before he could make up his mind to break in upon the little stock of provisions, which there was really more satisfaction in contemplating than in eating any ordinary supper. But the sight of some of his comrades resorting for solace to their rations decided him, and he shared with them the contents of his haversack.

The train reached Fall River at nine o'clock, and the passengers were transferred to the steamer

"Metropolis." The boat was soon swarming with soldiers, stacking their arms, and hurrying this way and that in the lamp-light. Then the clanking of the engine, the trembling of the steamer, and the sound of rushing water, announced that they were once more in motion.

Frank had never been on salt water before, and he was sorry this was in the night; but he was destined before long to have experience enough of the sea, both by night and by day.

When he went upon deck the next morning, the steamer was cutting her way gayly through the waters of New York harbor, — a wonderful scene to the un-travelled drummer boy, who had never before wit-nessed such an animated picture of dancing waters, ships under full sail, and steamboats trailing long dragon-tails of smoke in the morning air.

Then there was the city, with its forests of masts, its spires rising dimly in the soft, smoky atmosphere that shrouded it, and the far, faint sound of its bells musically ringing.

Then came the excitement of landing; the troops forming, and, after a patriotic reception by the "Sons of Massachusetts," marching through the city to the barracks; then dinner; and a whole afternoon of sight-seeing afterwards.

The next day the regiment was off again, crossing

the ferry, and taking the cars for Philadelphia. From Philadelphia it kept on into the night again, until it reached a steamer, in waiting to receive it, on Chesapeake Bay.

The next morning was rainy; and the rain continued all day, pouring dismally; and it was raining still when, at midnight, the boat arrived at Annapolis. In the darkness and storm the troops landed, and took up their temporary quarters in the Naval Academy. In one of the recitation halls, Frank and his comrades spread their blankets on the floor, put their knapsacks under their heads, and slept as soundly after their wearisome journey as they ever did in their beds at home. Indeed, they seemed to fall asleep as promptly as if by word of command, and to snore by platoons.

The next morning the rain was over. At seven o'clock, breakfast; after which the regiment was reviewed on the Academy parade. Then Frank and a squad of jovial companions set out to see the town, — taking care to have with them an intelligent young corporal, named Gray, who had been there before, and knew the sights.

"Boys," said young Gray, as they sallied forth, " we are now in Queen Anne's city, — for that, I suppose you know, is what the word Annapolis means. It was the busiest city in Maryland once; but, by degrees, all its trade and fashion went over to Baltimore, and left

the old town to go to sleep, — though it has woke up
and rubbed its eyes a little since the rebellion broke
out."

"When was you here, Gray?" asked Jack Winch.

Gray smiled at his ignorance, while Frank said, —

"What! didn't you know, Jack, he was here with
the Eighth Massachusetts, last April, when they
saved Washington and the Union?"

"The Union ain't saved yet!" said Jack.

"But we saved Washington; that's every where
admitted," said Gray, proudly. "On the 19th of
April the mob attacked the Sixth Massachusetts
in Baltimore, took possession of the city, and destroyed the communication with Washington. You
remember that, for it was the first blood shed in this
war; and April 19, 1861, takes its place with April 19,
1775, when the first blood was shed at Lexington, in
the Revolution."

"Of course I know all that!" said Jack, who never
liked to be thought ignorant of any thing.

"Well, there was the government at Washington in
danger, the Eighth Massachusetts on its way to
save it, and Baltimore in the hands of the rebels. I
tell you, every man of us was furious to cut our way
through, and avenge the murders of the 19th. But
General Butler hit upon a wiser plan, and instead
of keeping on to Baltimore, we switched off, seized a

ferry-boat on the Chesapeake, just as she was about to be taken by the secessionists, ran down here to Annapolis, saved the city, saved the old frigate 'Constitution,' and, with the New York Seventh, went to work to open a new route to Washington.

"Our boys repaired the railroad track, which the traitors had torn up, and put in shape again the engine they had disabled. We had men that could do any thing; and that very engine was one they had made, — for the South never did its own engine-building, but sent to Massachusetts to have it done. Charley Homans knew every joint and pin in that old machine, and soon had her running over the road again."

"How far is it to Washington?" asked Frank.

"About forty miles; but then we thought it a hundred, we were so impatient to get there! What a march we had! all day and all night, the engine helping us a little, and we helping the engine by hunting up and replacing now and then a stray rail which the traitors had torn from the track. A good many got used up, and Charley Homans took 'em aboard the train. It was on that march I fell in with one of the pleasantest fellows I ever saw; always full of wit and good-humor, with a cheery word for every body. He belonged to the New York Seventh. He told me his name was Winthrop. But I did not know till afterwards that he was Theodore Winthrop, the author; afterwards Major Winthrop, who fell last June — only two months after — at Big Bethel."

"It was a North Carolina drummer boy that shot him," said Frank. "Winthrop was heading the attack on the battery; he jumped upon a log, and was calling to the men, 'Come on!' when the drummer boy took a gun, aimed deliberately, and shot him dead."

"I wouldn't want to be killed by a miserable drummer boy!" said Jack Winch, envious because Frank remembered the incident.

"A drummer boy may be as brave as any body," said Frank, keeping his temper. "But I wouldn't want to be even the bravest drummer boy, in a bad cause."

"And as for being shot," said Gray, "I think Jack wouldn't willingly place himself where there was much danger of being killed by any body."

"You'll see! you'll see!" said Jack, testily. "Just wait till the time comes."

"What water is this the town fronts on?" asked Frank.

"The Chesapeake, of course! Who don't know that?" said Jack, contemptuously.

"Only it ain't!" said Gray, with a quiet laugh. "This is the River Severn. The Chesapeake is some two miles below."

"There, Jack," said Ned Ellis, "I'd give up now. You don't know quite so much as you thought you did."

"What a queer old town it is," said Frank, generously wishing to draw attention from Jack's mortification. "It isn't a bit like Boston. It don't begin to be as smart a place."

"Of course not!" said Jack, more eager than ever now to appear knowing. "And why should it be? Boston is the capital of Massachusetts; and if Annapolis was only the capital of this state, it would be smart enough."

"What is the capital of this state?" asked Gray, winking slyly at Frank.

"Baltimore! I thought every body knew that," said Jack, with an air of importance.

This ludicrous blunder raised a great laugh.

"O Jack! O Jack Winch! where did you go to school?" said Joe Harris, "not to know that Frederick is the capital of Maryland."

"So it is! I had forgotten," said Jack. "Of course I knew Frederick was the capital, if I had only thought."

At this the boys laughed louder than ever, and Jack flew into a passion.

"Harris was fooling you," whispered Frank.

8 *

"Annapolis is the capital. Gray is taking us now to see the State House."

"Ha, ha, ha!" Winch suddenly burst forth. "Did you think I didn't know? Annapolis is the capital; and there's the State House."

"Is it possible?" said Gray. "The rebels must have changed it then, for that was St. John's College when I was here before."

The boys shouted with merriment; all except Jack, who was angry. He had been as fickle at his studies, when at school, as he had always been at every thing else; never sticking long to any of them, but forever beginning something new; until, at last, ignorant of all, he gave up, declaring that he had knowledge enough to get through the world with, and that he wasn't going to bother his brain with books any longer. It added now to his chagrin to think that he had not education enough to prevent him from appearing ridiculous among his mates, and that the golden opportunity of acquiring useful information in his youth was lost forever.

Meanwhile Frank's reflections were very different. Gray's reminiscences of April had strongly impressed upon his mind the fact that he was now on the verge of his country's battle-fields; that this was the first soil that had been wrested from the grasp of treason, and saved for the Union, — that the ground he stood upon was already historic. And now the sight of some negroes reminded him that he was for the first time in his life in a *slave state.*

"These are the fellows that are the cause of this war," said Gray, indicating the blacks.

"Yes," said Winch, anxious to agree with him, "it's the abolitionists that have brought the trouble on the country. They insisted on interfering with the rights of the south, and so the south rebelled."

"We never interfered with slavery in the states where it belonged," said Frank, warmly. "The north opposed the extension of slavery over new territory, and took the power of the government out of the hands of the slaveholders, who had used it for their own purposes so long; and that is what made them rebel."

"Well, the north is partly to blame," insisted Jack, thinking he had Gray on his side.

"Yes; to blame for letting the slaveholders have their own way so long," said Frank. "And just as much to blame for this rebellion, as my father would be for my conduct, if he should attempt to enforce discipline at home, and I should get mad at it and set the house on fire."

"A good comparison," said Gray. "Because we were going to restore the spirit of the constitution, which is for freedom, and always was, though it has been obliged to tolerate slavery, the slaveholders, as Frank says, got mad and set Uncle Sam's house afire."

"He had heard somebody else say so, or he wouldn't have thought of it," said Jack, sullenly.

"No matter; it's true!" said Gray. "The south is fighting for slavery, — the corner-stone of the confederacy, as the rebel vice-president calls it, — while the north —— "

"We are fighting for the Constitution and the Union!" said Jack.

"That's true, too; for the constitution, as I said, means freedom; and now the Union means, union *without* slavery, since we have seen that union with slavery is impossible. We are fighting for the same thing our forefathers fought for — Liberty!"

"They won liberty for the whites only," said Frank. "Now we are going to have liberty for all men."

"If I had a brother that was a slaveholder and secessionist, I wouldn't say any thing," sneered Jack.

Frank felt cut by the taunt; but he said, gayly, —

"I won't spoil a story for relation's sake! Come, boys, politics don't suit Jack, so let's have a song; the one you copied out of the newspaper, Gray. It's just the thing for the occasion."

Frank's voice was a fine treble; Gray's a mellow

bass. Others joined them, and the party returned to the Academy, singing high and clear these words : —

> " The traitor's foot is on thy shore,
>   Maryland, my Maryland !
> His touch is on thy senate door,
>   Maryland, my Maryland !
> Avenge the patriotic gore
> That stained the streets of Baltimore,
> When vandal mobs our banners tore,
>   Maryland, my Maryland !
>
> " Drum out thy phalanx brave and strong,
>   Maryland, my Maryland !
> Drum forth to balance right and wrong,
>   Maryland, my Maryland !
> Drum to thy old heroic song,
> When forth to fight went Freedom's throng,
> And bore the spangled flag along,
>   Maryland, my Maryland ! "

" That's first-rate ! " said Frank, who delighted in music. " Gray altered the words a little, and Mr. Sinjin found us the tune."

" Frank likes any thing that has a drum in it," said John Winch, enviously. " He'll get sick of drums, though, soon enough, I guess."

" Jack judges me by himself," said Frank, gayly, setting out to run a race with Gray to the parade-ground.

IX.

THANKSGIVING IN CAMP.

Sт. Joнn's College stands on a beautiful eminence overlooking the city. The college, like the naval school, had been broken up by the rebellion; its halls and dormitories were appropriated to government uses, and the regiment was removed thither the next day.

"You will be surprised," Frank wrote home, "to hear that I have been through the naval school since I came here, and that I am now in college."

Few boys get through college as quick as he did. On the following day the regiment abandoned its new quarters also, and encamped two miles without the city. In the afternoon the tents were pitched; and where was only a barren field before, arose in the red sunset light the canvas city, with its regular streets, its rows of tent doors opening upon them, and its animated, laughing, lounging, working inhabitants.

The next morning was fine. All around the camp were pleasant growths of pine, oak, gum, and persimmon trees, and now and then a tree festooned with

wild grape-vines. Near by were a few scattered an-
cient-looking farm-houses, with their out-door chim-
neys, dilapidated out-buildings, negro huts, and tobacco
fields. There were several other regiments in the
vicinity, — two of Massachusetts boys. And there the
New York Zouaves, in their beautiful Oriental costumes, were encamped. Frank climbed a tree, and
looked far around on the picturesque and warlike
scene. The pickets, which had gone out the night before, now returning, discharged their loaded pieces at
targets, the reports blending musically with the near
and distant roll of drums.

"What is the cheering for?" asked Frank, as he
came in that day from a ramble in the woods.

"For General Burnside," said Gray. "All the troops
rendezvousing at Annapolis are to be under his command, to be called the Coast Division. It is to be
another Great Armada; and our colonel thinks we
shall see fighting soon."

This good news had made the regiment almost wild
with joy; for it desired nothing so much as to be led
against the enemy by some brave and famous general.

Frank loved the woods; and the next day he induced his companions to go with him and hunt for
nuts and fruits. Although it was late in autumn, there
were still persimmons and wild grapes to be had, and
walnuts, and butternuts. But Frank had another

object in view than that of simply pleasing his appetite. Thanksgiving day, which is bred in the bones of the New Englander, and which he carries with him every where, was at hand, and the drummer boy had thought of something which he fancied would suit well the festal occasion.

"What are you there after?" said John Winch, from a persimmon tree; "filling your hands with all that green stuff. Come here; O, these little plums are delicious, I tell you."

"These grapes are the thing," said Harris, from another tree. "I'm going to eat all I can; then I'm going to get my pockets full of nuts and carry back to camp."

Frank busied himself in his own way, however, and returned to camp with his arms loaded with evergreens.

"What in time are you about?" said Winch, as Frank set himself industriously to work with twigs and strings. "O, I know; wreaths! Boys, le's make some wreaths. Give me some of your holly, won't you, Frank?"

"Yes," said Frank, "take all you want to use. I shall be very glad to have you help me."

"Will you show me how?"

"Yes," said Frank; "sit down here. Bend your twigs and tie them together, in the first place, for a frame. Then bind the holly on it, this way."

"O, ain't it fun?" said Winch, with his usual enthusiasm over a new thing. "When we get these evergreens used up, we'll get some more, and make wreaths for all the tents." He worked for about ten minutes; then began to yawn. "Where's my pipe? I'm going to have a smoke. How can you have patience with that nonsense, Frank? What's the use of a wreath, anyhow, after it's made? Girl's play, I call it."

And off went Winch, having used up a ball of Frank's strings to no purpose, and leaving his wreath half finished.

But Frank, never easily discouraged, kept cheerfully at work, leaving his task only when duty called him.

Thursday came, — THANKSGIVING. A holiday in camp. The regiment had made ample preparations to celebrate it. Instead of pork and salt junk, the men were allowed turkeys; and in place of boiled hominy and molasses, they had plum pudding. And they feasted, and told gay stories, and sang brave songs, and thought of home, where parents, wives, sisters, and friends were, they fondly believed, eating turkey and plum pudding at the same time, and thinking of them. There was no drill that day; and no practise with any drumsticks but those of the devoted turkeys.

One of the most pleasing incidents of the day occurred in the morning. This was the presentation

7

of wreaths. Frank had made one for each of the company tents, and a fine one for Captain Edney, and one equally fine for Mr. Sinjin, the drum-major, and a noble one for the colonel of the regiment. He presented them all in person, except the last, which he requested Captain Edney to present for him. The captain consented, and at the head of a strong delegation of officers and men, proceeded to Colonel —— 's tent, called him out, and made a neat little speech, and presented the wreath on the end of his sword.

The colonel seemed greatly pleased.

" I accept this wreath," he said, "as the emblem of. a noble thought, which I am sure must have inspired our favorite young drummer boy in making it."

Frank blushed like a girl with surprise and pleasure at this unexpected compliment.

" The wreath," continued the colonel, "is the crown of victory; and we will hang up ours, my fellow-soldiers, on this memorable Thanksgiving day, as beautiful and certain symbols of the success of BURNSIDE'S EXPEDITION."

This short speech was greeted with enthusiastic applause. Frank was delighted with the result of his little undertaking, feeling himself a thousand times repaid for all his pains; while John Winch, seeing him in such high favor with every body, could not help regretting, with many a jealous pang, that he had not assisted in making the wreaths, and so become one of the heroes of the occasion.

That evening another incident occurred, not less pleasing to the drummer boy. With a block of wood for a seat, and the head of his drum for a desk, he was writing a letter to his mother, by a solitary candle, around which his comrades were playing cards on a table constructed of a rough board and four sticks. Amid the confusion of laughter and disputes, with heads or arms continually intervening between him and the uncertain light, he was pursuing his task through difficulties which would have made many a boy give up in vexation and despair, when a voice suddenly exclaimed, with startling emphasis, —

"Frank Manly, drummer!" And at the same instant something was thrown into the tent, like a bombshell, passing the table, knocking over the candle, and extinguishing the light.

"Well, that's manners, I should say," cried the voice of Seth Tucket, a fellow, as Frank described him, "who makes lots of fun for us, partly because he is full of it himself, and partly because he is green, and don't know any better." Tucket muttered and spat, then broke forth again, "I be darned ef that pesky football didn't take me right in the face, and spatter my mouth full of taller."

"Well, save the *taller*, Seth, for we're getting short

of candles," said Frank. "Here, who is walking on my feet?"

"It's me," said Atwater. "I'm going out to see who threw that thing in."

"You're too late," said Frank. "Strike a light, somebody, and let's see what it is. It tumbled down here by my drum, I believe."

There was a general scratching of matches, and after a while the broken candle was set up and re-lighted.

"I swan to man," then said Tucket, "jest look at that jack-of-spades. He got it in the physiognomy wus'n I did. 'Alas, the mother that him bare, if she had been in presence there, in his *greased cheeks* and *greasier hair*, she had not known her child.'"

These words from Marmion, aptly altered to suit the occasion, Seth, who was not so green but that he knew pages of poetry by heart, repeated in a high-keyed, nasal sing-song, which set all the boys laughing.

"A pretty way, too, to *turn up* Jack, I should say," he added, in allusion to the candlestick, — a *turnip* with a hole in it, — which had rolled over his cards.

In the mean time, Frank and Jack Winch were scrambling for the missile.

"Let me have it," snarled Jack.

"It's mine; my name was called when it was flung in," said Frank, maintaining his hold.

"Well, keep it, then!" said John. "It's nothing but a great wad of paper."

"It's a torpedo! an infernal machine!" cried Tucket. "Look out, Manly! it'll blow us all into the next Fourth of July."

Frank laughed, as he began to undo the package. The first wrapper was of brown paper with these words written upon it, in large characters: —

"FRANK MANLY, *Drummer.*
Inquire Within."

Beneath that wrapper was another, and beneath that another, and so on, apparently an endless series. The boys all gathered around Frank, looking on as he removed the papers one by one, until the package, originally as big as his head, had dwindled to the dimensions of his fist.

"It's got as many peels as an onion," said Tucket.

"Nothing but papers. I told ye so!" said Jack Winch.

But Frank perceived that the core of the package was becoming comparatively solid and weighty. There was certainly something besides paper there. What could it be? a stone? But what an odd-shaped stone it was! Stones are not often of such regular shape, so uniformly round and flattened. He had almost reached the last wrapper; his heart was beating anxiously; but, before he removed it, he thought he heard a peculiar sound, and held down his ear. A flush of delight overspread his countenance, and he clasped the ball in both hands, as if it had been something precious.

"O, boys!" he exclaimed, looking up eagerly for their sympathy, "where *did* it come from? Atwater, did you see any body?"

Nobody. It was all a mystery.

"Boys, it's for me, isn't it?" said Frank, still hugging his treasure, as if afraid even of looking at it, lest it should fly away.

"Come, let's see!" and Winch impatiently made a snatch to get at it.

Atwater coolly took him by the arm, and pulled him back. Then Frank, carefully as a young mother uncovers the face of her sleeping baby, removed the tinsel paper, which now alone intervened between the object and his hand, and revealed to the astonished eyes of his comrades a tiny, beautiful, smiling-faced silver watch.

"O, isn't it a beauty?" said Frank, almost beside himself with delight; for a watch was a thing of which he had greatly felt the need in beating his calls, and wished for in vain. "Who could have sent it? Don't you know, boys, any of you?" he asked, the mystery that came with the gift filling him with a strange, perplexed gladness.

"All I know is," said Tucket, "I'd be willing to have six candles, all lit, knocked down my throat, and eat taller for a fortnight, ef such a kind of a football, infernal machine, — *watch you call it*, — would only come to me."

"Frank 'll feel bigger 'n ever now, with a watch in his pocket," said the envious Jack Winch, with a bitter grin.

All had some remark to make except Atwater, who stood with his arms drawn up under his cape, and smiled down upon Frank well pleased.

Frank in the mean time was busily engaged in trying to discover, among all the papers, some scrap of writing by which the unknown donor might be traced. But writing there was none. And the mystery remained unsolved.

X.

FRANK'S PROGRESS.

So passed Thanksgiving in camp.

The next day the boys, with somewhat lugubrious faces, returned to their hard diet of pork and hominy, heaving now and then a sigh of fond remembrance, as they thought of yesterday's puddings and turkeys.

And now came other hardships. The days were generally warm, sometimes hot even, like those of July in New England. But the nights were cold, and growing colder and colder as the winter came on. And the tents were but a thin shelter, and clothing was scanty, and the men suffered. Many a time Frank, shivering under his blanket, thought, with a swelling and homesick heart, of Willie in his soft, warm bed, of his mother's inexhaustible store of comforters, and of the kitchen stove and the family breakfast, those raw wintry mornings.

From the day the regiment encamped, the men had expected that they were soon to move again. But now they determined that, even though they should have orders to march in three days, they would make themselves comfortable in the mean while. They accordingly set to work constructing underground stoves, covered with flat stones, with a channel on one side to convey away the smoke, and a deeper channel on the other for the draft. These warmed the earth, and kept up an even temperature in the tents all night.

I said Frank sometimes had homesick feelings. It was not alone the hardships of camp life that caused them. But as yet he had not received a single letter from his friends, and his longing to get news from them was such as only those boys can understand who have never been away from home until they have suddenly gone upon a long and comfortless journey, and who then begin to realize, as never before, all the loving care of their parents, the kindness of brothers and sisters, and the blessedness of the dear old nest from which they have untimely flown.

Owing to the uncertainty of the regiment's destination, Captain Edney had told his men to have all their friends' letters to them directed to Washington. There they had been sent, and there, through some misunderstanding or neglect, they remained. And though a small mail-bag full had been written to Frank, this was the reason he had never yet received one.

Alas for those missing letters! The lack of them injured Frank more deeply and lastingly than simply by wounding his heart. For soon that hurt began to heal. He was fast getting used to living without news from his family. He consoled himself by entering more fully than he had done at first into the excitements of the camp. And the sacred influence of HOME, so potent to solace and to save, even at a distance, was wanting.

And here begins a portion of Frank's history which I would be glad to pass over in silence. But, as many boys will probably read this story who are not altogether superior to temptation, and who do not yet know how easy it is for even a good-hearted, honest, and generous lad sometimes to forget his mother's lessons and his own promises, and commence that slow, gradual, downward course, which nearly always begins before we are aware, and from which it is then so hard to turn back; and as many may learn from his experience, and so save themselves much shame and their friends much anguish, it is better that Frank's history should be related without reserve.

In the first place, he learned to smoke. He began by taking a whiff, now and then, out of the pipe of a comrade, just to be in fashion, and to keep himself warm those chill evenings and mornings. Then a tobacco planter gave him, in return for some polite act on his part, a bunch of tobacco leaves, which Frank, with his usual ingenuity, made up into cigars for himself and friends. The cigars consumed, he obtained more tobacco of some negroes, addicted himself to a pipe, and became a regular smoker.

Now, I don't mean to say that this, of itself, was a very great sin. It was, however, a foolish thing in Frank to form at his age a habit which might tyrannize over him for life, and make him in the end, as he himself once said to John Winch, "a filthy, tobacco-spitting old man."

But the worst of it was, he had promised his mother he would not smoke. He thought he had a good excuse for breaking his word to her. "I am sure," he said, "if she knew how cold I am sometimes, she wouldn't blame me." Unfortunately, however, when one promise has been broken, and nobody hurt, another is broken so easily!

Ardent, sympathetic, fond of good-fellowship, Frank caught quickly the spirit of those around him. He loved approbation, and dreaded any thing that savored of ridicule. He disliked particularly the appellation of "the parson," which John Winch, finding that it annoyed him, used now whenever he wished to speak of him injuriously. Others soon fell into the habit of applying to him the offensive title, without

malice indeed, and for no other reason, I suppose, than
that nicknames are the fashion in the army. To call a
man simply by his honest name seems commonplace;
but to christen him the "Owl" if his eyes are big,
or "Old Tongs" if his legs are long, or "Step-
and-fetch-it" if he suffers himself to be made the
underling and catspaw of his comrades, — that is considered picturesque and amusing.

Frank would have preferred any of these epithets to
the one Winch had fastened upon him. Perhaps it
was to show how little he deserved it, that he made
his conduct appear as unclerical as possible — smoking, swaggering, and, I am sorry to add, swearing.
Imbibing unconsciously the spirit of his companions,
and imitating by degrees their habits and conversation, he became profane before he knew it, — excusing
himself on the plea that every body swore in the
army. This was only too near the truth. Men who
had never before indulged in profanity, now frequently
let slip a light oath, and thought nothing of it. For it
is one of the great evils of war that men, however
refined at home, soon forget themselves amid the hardships, roughness, and turbulence of a soldier's life. It
seems not only to disguise their persons, but their
characters also; so that those vices which would have
shocked them when surrounded by the old social influences appear rather to belong to their new rude, half-

barbarous existence. And we all know the pernicious effect when numbers of one sex associate exclusively together, unblessed by the naturally refining influence of the other.

Such being the case with men of years and respectability, we need not wonder that Frank should follow their example. Indeed, from the first, we had but one strong ground of hope for one so young and susceptible — that he would remember his pledges to his mother. These violated, the career of ill begun, where would he end?

Here, however, I should state that Frank never thought, as some boys do, that it is smart and manly to swear. Sometimes we hear a man talk, whom the vicious habit so controls that he cannot speak without blasphemy. With such, oaths become, as necessary a part of speech as articles or prepositions. If deprived of them they are crippled; they seem lost, and cannot express themselves. They are therefore unfit for any society but that of loafers and brawlers. Such slavery to an idle and foolish custom Frank had the sense to detest, even while he himself was coming under its yoke.

Here, too, before quitting the subject, justice requires us to bear witness in favor of those distinguished exceptions to the common profanity, all the more honorable because they were few. Although, generally speaking, officers and men were addicted to the practice, the language of here and there an officer, and here and there a private, shone like streaks of unsullied snow amid ways of trodden mire. Captain Edney never swore. Atwater never did. No profane word ever fell from the lips of young Gray. And there were others whose example in this respect was equally pure.

Fortunately, Frank was kept pretty busy these times; else, with that uneasy hankering for excitement which possesses unoccupied minds, and that inclination to mischief which possesses unoccupied hands, he might have acquired worse vices.

No doubt some of our young readers will be interested to know what he had to do. The following were some of his duties : —

At daybreak the *drummer's call* was beat by the drums of the guard-tent. Frank, though once so profound a sleeper, had learned to wake instantly at the sound ; and, before any of his comrades were astir, he snatched up his drum, and hurried from the tent. That call was a signal for all the drummers to assemble before the colors of the regiment, and beat the *reveille.* Then Frank and his fellow-drummers practised the *double-quick* for two hours. Then they beat the *breakfast call.* Then they ate their breakfast. At eight o'clock they had to turn out again, and beat the *sergeant's call.* At nine o'clock they beat for *guard mounting.* Then they practised two hours more at *wheeling, double-quick,* &c. They then beat the *dinner call.* Then they had the pleasure of laying aside the drumsticks, and taking up the knife and fork once more. After dinner more *calls* and similar practice. The time from supper (five o'clock) until the beat for the evening roll-call (at eight), the drummers had to themselves. After that the men were dismissed for the night, and could go to bed if they chose, — all except the drummers, who must sit up and beat the *tattoo* at nine. That is the signal for the troops to retire. Then come the *taps* (to extinguish lights), beat by each drummer in the company, going down the line of tents.

There were other calls besides those mentioned, such as the company *drill call,* the *adjutant's call, to the color,* &c., all of which were beat differently; so that, as you see, the drummer boy's situation was no sinecure.

He found his watch of great assistance to him, in giving him warning of the moment to be ready for the stated calls. Although evidently a new watch, it had been well regulated, and it kept excellent time. The secret donor of this handsome present was still undiscovered. Sometimes he suspected the colonel, sometimes Captain Edney; then he surmised that it

must somehow have come to him from home. But
all his conjectures and inquiries on the subject were
alike in vain; and he enjoyed the exquisite torment
of feeling that he had a lover somewhere who was
unknown to him.

XI.

A CHRISTMAS FROLIC.

CHRISTMAS came. The men had a holiday, but no turkeys, no plum puddings, except such as had come to individuals in private boxes from home. The sight of these boxes was not very edifying to those who had none. Frank, who was once more in communication with his friends, had expected such a box, and been disappointed.

"You jest come along with me, boys," said Seth Tucket, "and we'll lay in for as merry a Christmas as any of 'em. It may come a little later in the day; but patient waiters are no losers,—as the waiter said when he picked the pockets of the six gentlemen at dinner."

"What's the fun?" asked the boys, who were generally ready for any sport into which Seth would lead them.

He answered them enigmatically. "'*Evil, be thou my good!*'—that's what Milton's bad angel said. '*Fowl, be thou my fare!*'—that's what I say." From which significant response, followed by an apt imitation of a turkey gobbler, the boys understood that he had some device for obtaining poultry for dinner.

It was a holiday, as I have said, and they had already got permission to go beyond the lines. There were some twenty of them in all, Frank included. Tucket led them to a thicket about two miles from camp, where they halted.

"You see that house yonder. That's where old Buckley lives — the meanest man in Maryland."

"I know him," said Frank. "He's a rebel; he threatened to set his dog on us one day. He hates the Union uniform worse than he does the Old Scratch."

"He has got lots of turkeys," said Ellis, "which he told the sergeant he'd see die in the pen before he'd sell one to a Yankee."

"I know where the pen is," said John Winch; "he keeps 'em shut up, so our boys shan't steal 'em, and he and his dog and his nigger watch the pen."

"Well, boys," said Seth, "now the thing is to get the turkeys. As rebel property, it's our duty to confiscate 'em, and use 'em for the support of the Union cause. Now I've an idee. I'll go over in the woods there, and wait, while one of you goes to the house and asks him if he has got any turkeys to sell. He'll say no, of course. Then ask him if you may have the one out in the woods there. He'll say there ain't none in the woods; but you must insist there is one, and say if 'tain't his you'll take it, and settle with the owner when he calls. That'll start him, and I'll see that he goes into the woods fur enough, so that the rest of you can rush up, grab every man his turkey, and skedaddle. Winch 'll show you the way; he says he knows the pen. 'Charge, Ellis, charge! On, Harris, on! Shall be the words of private John.' But who'll go first to the house?" asked Seth, coming down from the high key in which he usually got off his poetry.

"Let Frank," said Harris; "for he knows the man."

"He? He dasn't go!" sneered Jack. "He's afraid of the dog."

This base imputation decided Frank to undertake the errand, which, after all, notwithstanding the danger attending it, was less repugnant to his feelings than more direct participation in the robbery.

Seth departed to ensconce himself in the woods. Frank then went on to the secessionist's house, quieting his conscience by the way with reflections like these: It was owing to such men as this disloyal Marylander that the Union troops were now suffering so many hardships. The good things possessed by traitors, or by those who sympathized with traitors, were fairly forfeited to patriots who were giving their blood to their country. Stealing, in such a case, was no robbery. And so forth, and so forth — sentiments which pre-

vailed pretty generally in the army.   Besides, there
was fun*in the adventure; and with boys a little fun
covers a multitude of sins.

The fun, however, was considerably dampened, on
Frank's part, as he approached the house. "Bow,
wow!" suddenly spoke the deep, dreadful tones of
the rebel mastiff. He hated the national uniform as
intensely as his master did, and came bounding towards Frank as if his intention was to eat him up
at once.

Now, the truth is, Frank was afraid of the dog.
His heart beat fast, his flesh felt an electric chill, and
there was a curious stirring in the roots of his hair.
The dog came right on, bristling up as large as two
dogs, opening his ferocious maw, and barking and
growling terribly. Then the fun of the thing was still
more dampened, to the boy's appreciation, by a sudden
suspicion. Why had his companions thrust the most
perilous part of the enterprise upon him, the youngest
of the party?   It was mean; it was cowardly; and the
whole affair was intended to make sport for the rest,
by getting him into a scrape. So, at least, thought
Frank.

"But I'll show them I've got some pluck," said
something within him, proud and determined.

To fear danger is one thing. To face it boldly, in
spite of that fear, is quite another. The first is com-

mon; the last is rare as true courage. The dog came straight up to Frank, and Frank marched straight up to the dog.

"Even if I had known he would bite," said Frank, afterwards, "I'd have done it." For he did not know at the time that this was the very best way to avoid being bitten. The dog, astonished by this straightforward proceeding, and probably thinking that one who advanced unflinchingly, with so brave a face, without weapons, must have honest business with his master, stepped aside, and growlingly let him pass.

"Where's your master?" said Frank, coolly, to an old negro, who was shuffling across the yard. "I want to see him a minute."

"Yes, massa," said the black, pulling at his cap, and bowing obsequiously.

He disappeared, and presently "old Buckley" came out, looking worthy to be the dog's master.

"Perhaps," thought Frank, "if I treat him in the same way, he won't bite, either;" and he walked straight up to him. The biped did not bark or growl, as the quadruped had done, but he looked wickedly at the intruder.

"How about those turkeys?" said Frank.

"What turkeys?" returned the man, surlily.

"It is Christmas now, and I thought you might be ready to sell some of them," continued Frank, nothing daunted.

"I've no turkeys to sell," said the man.

"But you had a lot of them," said Frank.

"I had fifty." Buckley looked sternly at Frank, and continued: "Half of them have been stolen by you Yankee thieves. And you know it."

"Stolen! If that isn't too bad!" exclaimed Frank. "I am sure I have never had one of them. Are you certain they have been stolen? I heard a gobbler over in the woods here, as I came along."

"You did?" said the man.

Frank thought it only a very white lie he was telling, having heard, at all events, a very good imitation of a gobbler. He repeated roundly his assertion. The man regarded him with a steady scowling scrutiny for near a minute, his surly lips apart, his hands thrust into his pockets. Frank, who could speak the truth with as clear and beautiful a brow as ever was seen, could not help wincing a little under the old fellow's slow, sullen, suspicious observation.

"Boy," said the man, without taking his hands from his pockets, "you're a lying to me!"

"Very well," said Frank, turning on his heel, "if you think so, then I suppose it isn't your turkey."

"And what are you going to do about it?" said the man.

"The federal army," said Frank, with a smile, "has need of that turkey. I shall take him, and settle with the owner when he turns up."

And he walked off. The man was evidently more than half convinced there was a turkey in the woods — probably one that had escaped when a part of his flock was stolen.

"Toby," said he, "fetch my gun."

The old negro trotted into the house, and trotted out again, bringing a double-barrelled shot-gun, which Frank did not like the looks of at all.

"There's some Yankee trick here," said the secessionist, cocking the piece, and carefully putting a cap on each barrel; "but I reckon they'll find me enough for 'em. Toby, you stay here with the dog, and take care of things. Now, boy, march ahead there, and show me that gobbler."

The old negro grinned. So did his master, in a way Frank did not fancy. It was a morose, menacing, savage grin — a very appropriate prelude, Frank thought, to a shot from behind out of that two-barrelled fowling-piece. But it was too late now to retreat. So, putting on a bold and confident air, he started for the woods, followed by the grim man with the gun.

His sensations by the way were not greatly to be envied. He had never felt, as he afterwards expressed it, so *streakéd* in his life. By that term I suppose he alluded to those peculiar thrills which sometimes creep over one, from the scalp to the ankles, when some great danger is apprehended. For it was evident that this man was in deadly earnest. Tramp, tramp, he came after Frank, with his left hand on the stock of his gun, the other on the lock, ready to pop him over the moment he should discover he had been trifled with. No doubt their depart-ure had been watched by the boys from the thicket, and the unlucky drummer expected every moment to hear the alarm of a premature attack upon the turkey-pen, which would, unquestionably, prove the signal for his own immediate execution.

"He will shoot me first," thought Frank, "to be revenged; then he'll run back to defend his prop-erty."

And now, although he had long since made up his mind that he was willing to die, if necessary, fighting for his country, his whole soul shrunk with fear and dread from the shameful death, in a shameful cause, with which he was menaced.

"*Shot, by a secessionist, in the act of stealing tur-keys.*" How would that sound, reported to his friends at home?

"*Shot while gallantly charging the enemy's battery.*" How differently that would read! and the poor boy wished that he had let the miserable turkeys alone, and waited to try his fortunes on the battle-field.

However, being once in the scrape, although the

cause was a bad one, he determined to show no craven spirit. With a heart like hot lead within him, he marched with every appearance of willingness and confidence into the woods, regarding the gun no more than if it had been designed for the obvious purpose of shooting the gobbler.

"When we come in sight of him," said Frank, "let me shoot him, won't you?"

"H'm! I reckon I'll give you a shot!" muttered the man, with darkly dubious meaning.

"I wish you would," said Frank. "Our boys have two cartridges apiece given them every day now, and they practise shooting at a target. But as I am a drummer, I don't have any chance to shoot. There's your turkey now."

In fact an unmistakable gobble was just then heard farther on in the woods.

"May I take the gun and go on and shoot him?" Frank asked, with an innocent air.

And he stopped, determined now to get behind the man, if he could not obtain the gun.

The rebel laughed grimly at the idea of giving up his weapon. But the sound of the turkey, together with the boy's cool and self-possessed conduct, had so far deceived him that he no longer drove Frank inexorably before him, but permitted him to walk by his side, and even to lag a little behind.

"Gobble, obble, obble!" said the turkey, behind some bushes, still several rods off.

"Yes, that's my turkey!" said the man, ready enough to claim the unseen fowl.

"How do you know he is yours?" asked Frank.

"I know his gobble. One I had stole gobbled jest like that." And the secessionist's stern features relaxed a little.

Frank's relaxed a little, too; for, serious as his dilemma had seemed a minute since, he could not but be amused by the man's undoubting recognition of *that* gobble.

"All turkeys make a noise alike," said Frank.

"No they don't, no they don't!" said the man, positively,—no doubt fearing a plot to get the fowl away from him, and anxious to set up his claim in season. "I reckon I know about turkeys. Hear that?"—as the sound was heard again, still at a distance. "That's my bird. I should know that gobble among five hundred."

Frank suppressed his merriment, thinking that now was his time to get away.

"Well," said he, "unless you'll sell me the bird, I don't know that there's any use of my going any farther with you."

He expected a repetition of the refusal to sell, when he would have the best excuse in the world for making

his escape. But Buckley was still suspicious of some trick, — fearing, perhaps, that Frank would run off and get help to secure the turkey.

"We'll see; we'll see. Wait till we get the bird," said the man. "You've done me a good turn telling me about him, and mayhap I'll sell him to you for your honesty. But wait a bit; wait a bit."

They were fast approaching the bushes where the supposed turkey was.

"Quit, quit, quit! Gobble, obble, obble!" said the pretended fowl.

"He *must* know now," thought Frank, with renewed apprehension; but he dared not run.

In fact, the old fellow was beginning to see that his recognition of *his* gobbler had been premature. A patch of blue uniform was visible through the brush. The rebel stopped, and drew up his gun. As Hamlet killed Polonius for a rat, so would he kill a Yankee for a turkey. Click! the piece was cocked and aimed.

"Here, you old clodhopper, you; don't you shoot! don't you shoot!" screamed Seth Tucket, rushing wildly out of the bushes just as the rebel pulled the trigger.

XII.

THE SECESSIONIST'S TURKEYS.

In the mean time the boys, watching from their ambush, and seeing that the rebel had gone off with Frank, but left his dog and negro behind, armed themselves with clubs. When all was ready, Winch gave the word, and forward they dashed at the double-quick, clearing more than half the space intervening between them and the barns, before they were discovered by the enemy. Then the dog bounded out with a bark, and the old negro began to "holler," and the rebel's wife and daughter ran out and screamed, and an old negress also appeared, brandishing a broom, and adding her voice to the chorus.

At this moment the report of a gun came from the direction in which the secessionist had gone off with Frank.

John Winch heard it, just as the dog met the charging party. Who was killed? Frank or Seth? John did not know, but he was frightened. He had come for fun and poultry, not for fighting and bullets. Neither was he particularly ambitious to be bitten by that monstrous dog. He lost faith in his club, and dropped it. He lost confidence in the prowess of his companions, and deserted them. In short, Jack Winch, who had been one of the most eager to engage in the adventure, took ignominiously to his heels.

He reached the thicket before venturing to look behind him. Then he saw that his comrades had frightened away the negro, beaten back the dog, and taken the turkey-pen by storm. He would now have been but too glad to join them; but it was too late. Having accomplished their undertaking, they were returning, each bringing, pendent by the legs, a flopping fowl.

It is better to be a brave man than a coward, even in a bad cause. Fortune often favors brave men in the wrong in preference to aiding cowards in the right, for Fortune loves not a poltroon. John Winch felt at that moment that nobody henceforth would love or favor him, and he began to frame excuses for his shameful conduct.

"Hello, Jack Winch," cried Ellis, coming up with a turkey in one hand and a chicken in the other, "you're a smart leader — to run away from a yelping dog like that!"

"Coward! coward!" chimed in the others, with angry contempt.

"I sprained my ankle. Didn't you know it?" said the miserable Jack, with a writhing countenance, limping.

"Sprained your granny!" exclaimed Harris. "I never saw a sprained ankle go over the ground so fast as yours did, just as we came to the dog."

"Then I heard the gun," said Jack, "and I was afraid either Seth or Frank was shot."

"Woe to the man of turkeys if they are!" said Joe, twisting the neck of his fowl to quiet it. "We'll serve him as I am serving this hen."

The boys hastened to a rendezvous they had appointed with the absent ones, followed by Jack at a very creditable pace, considering his excruciating lameness.

As yet, neither Frank nor Seth had been shot. The charge of buck shot fired from the rebel fowling-piece had entered the bushes just as the blue uniform left them. But the secessionist cocked the other barrel of his piece immediately, with the intention of making up for the error of his first aim.

"Shoot me," shouted Seth, "and you'll be swinging from that limb in five minutes!"

The man hesitated, glancing quickly about for those who were expected to put Seth's threat into execution.

"I've twenty fellows with me," added Setn, "and they'll string you up in no time, by darn!"

The secessionist was not so much impressed by the rather slender oath with which Seth clinched his speech, as by the sharp and earnest tone in which the whole was uttered, — Seth walking savagely up to him as he spoke. All the while, the alarm raised by the negro, and the dog, and the women, was sounding in the man's ears.

"They're after my turkeys! This is your trick, boy!" and he sprang upon Frank, lifting his gun as if to level him to the earth.

But Seth sprang after him, and seized the weapon before it descended. That green down-easter was cool as if he had been at a game of ball. He was an athletic youth, and he readily saw that Buckley, though a sturdy farmer, was no match for him. He pushed him back, shouting shrilly, at the same time, in the words of his favorite poet, —

"'Now, if thou strik'st him but one blow, I'll hurl thee from the brink as far as ever peasant pitched a bar!'"

This strange form of salutation astonished the rebel even more than the rough treatment he received at the hands of the vigorous and poetical Tucket. He saw that it was no time to stay and parley. He knew that his turkeys were going, and, muttering a parting malediction at Frank, he set off at a run to protect his poultry-yard.

"Now's our time," said Tucket, starting for the rendezvous, and striking into another quotation from his favorite minstrel, parodied for the occasion. "'Speed, Manly, speed! the cow's tough hide on fleeter foot was never tied. Speed, Manly, speed! such cause of haste a drummer's sinews never braced. For turkey's doom and rebel deed are in thy course — speed, Manly, speed!'"

And speed they did, arriving at the place of meeting just as their companions came up with the poultry.

"Hello, Jack!" said Frank; "what's the matter with you?"

"He stumbled over a great piece of bark," Ellis answered for Winch.

"Did you, Jack?"

"Yes!" said Jack, putting on a look of anguish. He had not thought of the bark before, but supposing Ellis had seen such a piece as he spoke of, he accepted his theory of the stumbling as readily as the rebel had recognized in Seth's gobbling one of his own lost turkeys. "And broke my ankle," added Jack.

"What kind of bark was it? do you know?" said Ellis.

"No. I was hurt so I didn't stop to look."

"Well, I'll tell you. It was the dog's bark." And

Ellis and his comrades shouted with laughter, all except poor Jack Winch, who knew too well that no other kind of bark had checked his progress.

Then the turkey-stealers had their adventure to relate, and Frank had his amusing story to tell, and Tucket could brag how near he had come to being shot for one of Buckley's gobblers, and all were merry but Jack, who had brought from the field nothing but a counterfeit lameness and dishonor, and who accordingly lagged behind his comrades, sulky and dumb.

"He limps dreadfully — when any body is looking at him," said Harris.

"Nobody killed, and only one wounded," said Frank.

"The sight of old Buckley coming with his dog would be better than a surgeon, to cure that wound," said Tucket. "You'd see Winch leg it faster 'n any of us — like the old woman that had the hypo's, and hadn't walked a step for twenty years, and thought she couldn't; but one day her friends got up a ghost to scare her, and she ran a mile before they could ketch her."

Do you know how these jokes, and the laughter that followed, sounded on the ear of Jack Winch? Even the bark of the rebel mastiff was music in comparison, and his bite would have hurt him less.

9

"By the way," said Seth, "the old skinflint will be after us, sure as guns. Hurry! or we'll hear — 'The deep-mouthed bull-dog's heavy bay resounding up the rocky way, and faint, from farther distance borne, the darned old rebel's dinner horn.' Give me that chicken, Ellis. And, boys, we must manage some way to smuggle these fowls into camp. I can carry this chicken under my coat; but how in Sam Hill you'll manage with the turkeys, I don't see."

"I know," said Frank, always full of invention. "If nobody else has a better plan, I've thought of a good one."

Several devices were suggested, but none met with general approbation. Then Frank explained his.

" Cover up the turkeys with evergreens, and we will go in with our arms full, as if we were going to make wreaths for the regiment."

This plan was agreed upon, and shortly after the adventurers might have been seen returning to camp loaded down with boughs and vines. Jack alone came in empty-handed. Frank had no turkey, and so he threw down his load outside the tent, where any one could examine it.

It was not long before the owner of the turkeys made his appearance, carrying to headquarters his complaint of the robbery. Unfortunately, Frank was not only known as a drummer boy, but he wore the letter of his company on his cap. Besides, his youth rendered his identification comparatively easy. As might have been expected, therefore, he was soon called to an account. Captain Edney himself came to investigate the matter, accompanied by the secessionist.

"That's the boy," said Buckley, with determined vindictiveness, when Frank was arraigned before him.

Frank could not help looking a little pale, for he felt that he was in a bad scrape, and how he was to get out of it, without either lying or betraying his accomplices, he could not see. He did not care so much about himself, but he would not for any thing have borne witness against the others. He had almost made up his mind to tell a sturdy falsehood, if necessary, — to stoop to a dishonorable thing in order to avoid another, which he considered even more damaging to his character. For such is commonly the result of wrong-doing; one step taken, you must take another to retrieve that. One foot in the mire, you must put the other in to get that out.

However, the drummer boy still hoped that by putting a bold face on the matter, and prevaricating a little, he might still keep clear of that thing he had been taught always to abhor — a downright untruth.

"This man brings serious charges against you, Frank," said Captain Edney.

"I should think it was for me to bring charges against him," replied Frank, trying to look indignant.

"Why, what has he done to you?" The captain could not help smiling as he spoke, and Frank felt encouraged.

"He's a rebel of the worst kind. He is always insulting the federal uniform, and he seems to think that whoever wears it is a villain. He threatened to set his dog on me the other day, and to-day he was going to knock me down with his gun."

"What was he going to knock you down for? You must have done something to provoke him."

"Yes, I did!" said Frank, boldly. "I went to his house, and asked him, in the politest way I could, if he would sell us fellows a turkey. I might have known that it would provoke him, for he has been heard to say he'd rather his turkeys should die in the pen than that a Union soldier should have one, even for money."

It was evident to the secessionist that instead of making out a case against the boy, the boy was fast making out a case against him. In his impatience he broke forth into violent denunciations of Frank, but Captain Edney stopped him.

"None of that, sir, or I'll send you out of the camp forthwith. He says," — turning to Frank, — "that you decoyed him into the woods while your companions stole his turkeys."

"Decoyed him?" said Frank. "He may call it what he pleases. I'll tell you just what I did, sir. He said he hadn't any turkeys. So I said, 'Then the one I heard in the woods, as I came along, isn't yours — is it?'"

"Had you heard one?"

"I had heard a noise so much like one," — laughing, — "that he himself, when he heard it, was ready to swear it was his gobbler."

"And was it really a turkey?"

"No, sir. It was Seth Tucket hid behind the bushes."

Frank was now conscious of making abundant fun for his comrades, who all crowded around, listening with delight to the investigation. Even Captain Edney smiled, as he gave a glance at the green-looking, seriously-winking Seth.

"So it was you that played the gobbler, Tucket," said the captain.

"I hope there wan't no great harm in't ef I did, sir," replied Seth, with ludicrous mock solemnity. "Bein' Christmas so, I thought I'd like a little bit of turkey, sir, ef 'twant no more than the gobble. And there I was, enjoying it all by myself, hevin' a nice time, when this man comes up and lays claim to me for his turkey."

This sober declaration, uttered in a high key, with certain jerks of the arms and twists of the down-east features, which Seth could use with the drollest effect, excited unrestrained mirth among the men, and made the officer's sword-belts shake not a little with the suppressed merriment inside.

"What do you mean by his claiming you?" asked the captain.

"He told Manly I belonged to him, and that some thieving Yankee had stolen me," said Seth, with open eyes and mouth, as if he had been making the most earnest statement. "Now I'll leave it to any body ef that's so. And I guess that's about all his complaints of hevin' turkeys stole amounts to; for ef he can make a mistake so easy in my case, he may in others. Though mabby he means I stole the *gobble* of one of his turkeys. I own it's a gobble I picked up somewheres, but I didn't know 'twas his." And Tucket drew down his face with an expression of incorruptible innocence.

"Well, boys," said the captain, silencing the laughter, "we have had fun enough for the occasion, though it *is* a merry Christmas. No more buffoonery, Tucket. Were you aware, Frank, that it was Tucket, and not a turkey, in the bushes, when you took this man to the woods?"

"I rather thought it was Tucket," said Frank, "though the man stuck to it so stoutly that 'twas his gobbler, I didn't know but —— "

"Never mind about that." The captain saw that it was Frank's object to lead the inquiry back to the ludicrous part of the business, and promptly checked him. "What was your motive in deceiving him?"

"To have a little fun, sir."

"Did you not know that there was a design to rob his poultry pen?"

Frank recollected his momentary doubts as to the good faith of his companions, when the dog assailed him, and thought he could make that uncertainty the base of a strong "No, sir."

"But you know his pen was robbed?"

"No, sir, I do not know it —," Frank reflecting as he spoke, that a man cannot really *know* any thing of which he has not been an eye-witness, and comforting his conscience with the fact that he had not *seen* the turkeys stolen.

"Now," — Captain Edney did not betray by look or word whether he believed or doubted the boy's assertion, — "tell me who was with you in the woods."

"Seth Tucket, sir."

"Who else?"

"O, ever so many fellows had been with me."

"Name them."

And Frank proceeded to name several who had really been with him that morning, but not on the forage after poultry. On being called up and questioned, they were able to give the most positive testimony, to the effect that they had neither stolen any fowls themselves nor been with any party that had. In the mean time the sergeant and second lieutenant instituted a search through the company's tents, and succeeded in finding a solitary turkey, which nobody could give any account of, and which nobody claimed. This the secessionist identified; averring that there were also a dozen more, besides several chickens, for which redress was due. But not one of them could be discovered, perhaps because they were so skilfully concealed, but more probably because those who searched were not anxious to find.

Captain Edney accordingly paid the man for the loss of the single turkey, which he ordered sent immediately to the hospital. He also told the secessionist that he would pay him for all the poultry he was ready to swear had been appropriated by the men of his company, provided he would first take the oath of allegiance to the United States. This Buckley sullenly refused to do, and he was immediately conducted by a guard outside the lines. Seth Tucket followed at a short distance, saying, as he put his hand in his pocket, as if to produce some money, "Say, friend! better le' me pay ye for that gobble I stole. Any thing in reason, ye know."

But Buckley gave him only a glance of compressed rage, and marched off in silence, with disappointment and revenge in his heart.

XIII.

THE EXPEDITION MOVES.

Frank won the greatest credit from his comrades by the manner in which he had gone through the investigation. And the fowls, which those who searched could not discover, found their way somehow to the cooks, and back again to the boys, and were shared among their companions, who had a feast and a good time generally.

But when all was over, and the excitement which carried Frank through had subsided, and it was night, and he lay in the darkness and solitude of the tent, with his comrades asleep around him, — then came sober reflection; and he thought of the poor man who had lost his turkeys, and who, for one, had got no fun out of the business; and he remembered that he had, to all intents and purposes, lied to Captain Edney; and he knew in his heart that he had done a dishonest thing.

Yes, he had actually been engaged in stealing turkeys. He was guilty of an act of which, a few weeks

(138)

before, he would have deemed himself absolutely incapable. All the mitigating circumstances of the case, which had lately stood out so clear and strong as almost to hide the offence from his moral vision, now faded, and shrunk away, and the wrong itself stood forth, alone, in its undisguised ugliness.

"What is it to me that the man is a secessionist? That doesn't give us the right to rob him. He is not in arms against the government; and we don't know that he assists the rebels in any way, either by giving them information or money. Perhaps he had good reason to hate the Union soldiers. If he had not before, he has now. I wish I had let his turkeys alone."

These words Frank did not exactly frame to himself, lying there in the dark and silent tent; but so said the soul within him. And the next day the culpability of his conduct was brought home still more forcibly to his conscience by the receipt of a box from home. It contained, besides a turkey, pies, cakes, apples, and letters. And in one of the letters his mother wrote, —

"I hope these things will reach you by Christmas, and that you will enjoy them, and share them with those who have been good to you, and be very happy. We all think of the hardships you have to go through, and would willingly give up many of our comforts if you could only have them. We shall not have

any turkey at Christmas — we shall all be so much
happier to think you have one. For I would not have
you so much as *tempted* to do what you say some of
the soldiers have done — that is, steal the turkeys
belonging to the secessionists. If there are rebels at
heart, not yet in open opposition to the government,
I would have you treat them kindly, and not provoke
them to hate our cause worse than they do already.
And always remember that, whatever the government
may see fit to do to punish such men, you have no
right to interfere with either their private opinions or
their private property."

Why was it that the contents of Frank's Christmas
box did not taste so good to him as he had anticipated? Simply because he could partake of neither
pie nor turkey without the sorry sauce of a reproving
conscience.

He thought to atone for his fault by magnanimity
in sharing with others what he could not relish alone.
He gave liberally to all his mates, and carried a large
piece of the turkey, together with a generous supply
of stuffing, and an entire mince pie, to his old friend
Sinjin.

Now, Frank had not, for the past month, been on
as good terms with the veteran as formerly. The
meeting with Mrs. Manly in Boston seemed to have
awakened unpleasant remembrances in the old drum-

mer's mind, and to render him unpleasantly stiff and cold towards her son. He had received the thanksgiving wreath with a very formal and stately acknowledgment, and Frank, who knew not what warm torrents might be gushing beneath the stern old man's icy exterior, had kept himself somewhat resentfully aloof from him ever since. But he still felt a yearning for their former friendship, and he now hoped, with the aid of the good gifts of which he was the bearer, to make up with him.

"I wish you a merry Christmas," said Frank, arrived at the old man's tent.

"You are rather late for that, it seems to me," replied Sinjin, lifting his brows, as he sat in his tent and looked quietly over his shoulder at the visitor.

"I know it," said Frank. "But the truth is, I hadn't any thing to wish you a merry Christmas with yesterday. But this morning I got a box by express, full of goodies, direct from home."

"Ah!" said the old man, with a singular unsteadiness of eye, while he tried to look cold and unconcerned.

"Yes; isn't it grand? A turkey of my mother's own stuffing, and pies of her own baking, and every thing that's splendid. And she said she hoped you would accept a share, with her very kind regards. And so I've brought you some."

The old man had got up on his feet. But he did not offer to relieve Frank's hands. He made no reply to his little speech; and he seemed not so much to look *at* him, as *through* him, into some visionary past far away. Perhaps it was not the drummer boy he saw at all, but fairer features, still like his — a sweet young girl; the same he used to trot upon his knees, in those unforgotten years, so long ago, when he was in his manhood's prime, and life was still fresh to him, and he had not lost his early faith in friendship and love.

There Frank stood, holding the cover of the Christmas box, with the good things from home upon it, and waited, and wondered; and there the old man stood and dreamed.

"Please, sir, will you let me leave them here?" said Frank, ready to cry with disappointment at this strange reception.

The old man heaved a sigh, brushed his hand across his eyes, and came back to the present. He stooped and took the gift with a tremulous smile, but without a word. He did not tell the drummer boy that he had, in that instant of forgetfulness, seen his mother as she was at his age, and that his old heart now, though seemingly withered and embittered, gushed again with love so sorrowful and yearning, that he could have taken her son in his arms, even as he had so often taken her, and have wept over him. And Frank, in his ignorance, went away, feeling more hurt than ever at his old friend's apparent indifference.

And now matters were assuming a more and more warlike appearance. For some time Frank's regiment had been out on brigade drill twice a week, and he had written home a glowing description of the scene. But an incomparably grander sight was the inspection and review of the entire division, which took place the last week of December. The parade ground, comprising two thousand acres, at once smooth and undulating, was admirably fitted to show off, with picturesque and splendid effect, the evolutions of regiment, brigade, and division. Thousands of spectators flocked from Annapolis and the vicinity, in vehicles, on horseback, and on foot, to witness the display.

Frank was with his company, carrying his knapsack, haversack, tin cup, and canteen, like the rest, and with his drum at his side. He could not but feel a pride in the grand spectacle of which he formed a part. At eleven o'clock, Brigadier-General Foster, commanding the department in Burnside's absence, passed down the line, accompanied by a numerous staff, and followed by the governor of the state and members of the legislature. They inspected each regiment in

turn ; and many were the looks of interest and pleased
surprise which the young drummer boy received from
officers and civilians.

The reviewing party then took its position on the
right, the words of command rang along the line, and
regiment after regiment, breaking into battalion column, filed, with steady tramp, in superb, glittering
array, to the sound of music, past the general and his
assistants. No wonder the drummer boy's heart beat
high with military enthusiasm, as he marched with his
comrades in this magnificent style, marvelling what
enemy could withstand such disciplined masses of
troops.

And now the fleet of transports, which were to convey them to their destination, were gathering at Annapolis. The camp was full of rumors respecting the
blow which was to be struck, and the troops were
eager to strike it.

So ended the old year, the first of the war; and the
new year came in. It was now January, 1862.

On the 3d, the regiment was for the first time paid
off. Frank received pay for two months' service, at
twelve dollars a month. He kept only four dollars for
his own use, and sent home the remaining twenty dollars in a check, to be drawn by his father in Boston.
It was a source of great pride and satisfaction to him
that he could send money to his parents; and he won-

dered at the greedy selfishness of John Winch, who immediately commenced spending his pay for pies and cakes, at the sutler's enormous prices.

On the 6th, the regiment broke camp and marched to Annapolis. There was snow on the ground, which had fallen the night before; and the weather was very cold. The city was a scene of busy activity. The fleet lay in the harbor. Troops and baggage trains crowded to the wharves. Transport after transport took on board its precious freight of lives, and hauling out into the stream to make room for others, dropped anchor off the town.

After waiting five hours — five long and dreary hours — at the Naval Academy, our regiment took its turn. One half went on board an armed steamer, whose decks were soon swarming with soldiers and bristling with guns. The other half took passage in a schooner. And the steamer took the schooner in tow, and anchored with her in the river. And so Frank and his comrades bade farewell to the soil of Maryland.

The excitement of these scenes had served to put Frank's conscience to sleep again. However, it received a sting, when, on the day of leaving Annapolis, he learned that the secessionist whose turkeys had been stolen, had, in revenge for his wrongs, quitted his farm, and gone to join the rebel army.

10

XIV.

THE VOYAGE AND THE STORM.

On the morning of the 9th of January the fleet sailed.

Frank was on board the schooner towed out by her steam consort.

Although the morning was cold and wet, the decks of the transports were crowded with troops witnessing the magnificent spectacle of their own departure.

Just before they got under way, a jubilant cheering was heard. Frank made his way to the vessel's side, to see what was going on. A small row-boat passed, conveying some officer of distinction to his ship. Frank observed that he was a person of quite unpretending appearance, but of pleasant and noble features.

"Burnside! Burnside! Burnside!" shouted a hundred voices.

And in acknowledgment of the compliment, the modest hero of the expedition stood up in the boat, and uncovered his high, bald forehead and dome-like head.

The rowers pulled at their oars, and the boat dashed on over the dancing waters, greeted with like enthusiasm every where, until the general's flag-ship, the little steamer Picket, took him on board.

And now the anchors were up, the smoke-pipes trailed their cloudy streamers on the breeze, flags and pennants were flying, paddle-wheels began to turn and plash, the bands played gay music, and the fleet drew off, in a long line of countless steamers and sailing vessels, down the Severn, and down the Chesapeake.

All day, through a cold, drizzling rain, the fleet sailed on, the transports still keeping in sight of each other, in a line extending for miles along the bleak, inhospitable bay.

The next morning, Frank went on deck, and found the schooner at anchor in a fog. The steamer lay alongside. No other object was visible — only the restlessly-dashing waters. The wild shrieking of the steamer's whistle, blowing in the fog to warn other vessels of the fleet to avoid running down upon them, the near and far responses of similarly screaming whistles, and of invisible tolling bells, added impressiveness to the situation.

At nine o'clock, anchors were weighed again, and

the fleet proceeded slowly, feeling its way, as it were,
in the obscurity. There was more or less fog through-
out the day; but towards sundown a breeze blew
from the shore, the fog rolled back upon the sea, the
clouds broke into wild flying masses, the blue sky
shone through, and the sunset poured its placid glory
upon the scene.

Again the troops crowded the decks. The fleet was
entering Hampton Roads. Upon the right, basking
in the golden sunset as in the light of an eternal calm,
a stupendous fortress lay, like some vast monster of
old time, asleep. Frank shivered with strange sensations as he gazed upon that immense and powerful
stronghold of force; trying to realize that, dreaming
so quietly there in the sunset, those gilded walls,
which seemed those of an ancient city of peace, meant
horrible, deadly war.

"By hooky!" said Seth Tucket, coming to his side,
"that old Fortress Monroe's a stunner — ain't she?
I'd no idee the old woman spread her hoop skirts over
so much ground."

"You can see the big Union gun there on the
beach," said Atwater. "To look at that, then just
turn your eye over to Sewell's Point there, where the
rebel batteries are, makes it seem like war." And the
tall, grave soldier smiled, with a light in his eye Frank
had seldom seen before.

The evening was fine, the sky clear, the moon shining, the air balmy and spring-like. The fleet had come to anchor in the Roads. The bands were playing, and the troops cheering from deck to deck. The moonlight glittered on the water, and whitened the dim ships riding at anchor, and lay mistily upon the bastions of the great slumbering fortress. At a late hour, Frank, with his eyes full of beauty and his ears full of music, went below, crept into his birth, and thought of home, and of the great world he was beginning to see, until he fell asleep.

The next day the fleet still lay in Hampton Roads. There were belonging to the expedition over one hundred and twenty-five vessels of all classes, freighted with troops, horses, forage, and all the paraphernalia of war. And this was the last morning which was to behold that magnificent and powerful armada entire and unscattered.

At night the fleet sailed. Once at sea, the sealed orders, by which each vessel was to shape its course, were opened, and Hatteras Inlet was found to be its first destination.

The next day was Sunday, January 12. The morning was densely foggy. Frank, who had been seasick all night, went on deck to breathe the fresh sea air. The steamer, still towing the schooner, was just visible in the fog, at the other end of the great sagging hawser. And the sea was rolling, rolling, rolling. And the ship was tossing, tossing, tossing. And Frank's poor stomach, not satisfied with its convulsive efforts to turn him wrong side out the night before, recommenced heaving, heaving, heaving. He clung to the rail of the schooner, and every time it went down, and every time it came up, he seemed to grow dizzier and sicker than ever. He consoled himself by reflecting that he was only one of hundreds on board, who were, or had been, in the same condition; and when he was sickest he could not help laughing at Seth Tucket's inexhaustible drollery.

"Well, try again, ef ye want to," said that poetical private, addressing his stomach. "Be mean, and stick to it. Keep heaving, and be darned!"

Stomach took him at his word, and for a few minutes he leaned heavily by Frank's side.

"There!" he said to it, triumphantly, "ye couldn't do any thing, and I told ye so. Now I hope ye'll keep quiet a minute. Ye won't? Going at it again? Very well; do as you please; it's none o' my business — by gosh!" — lifting up his head with a bitter grin; "that inside of me is like Milton's chaos, in Paradise Lost. 'Up from the bottom turned by raging wind and furious assault!' — Here it goes again!"

Frank had been scarcely less amused by the misery

of Jack Winch, who declared repeatedly that he should die, that he wished he was dead, and so forth, with groanings unutterable.

But Frank kept up his courage, and after eating a piece of hard bread for breakfast, began to feel better.

Towards noon the fog blew off, and the beach was visible on the right, — long, low, desolate, a shore of interminable sand, over which the breakers leaped and ran like hordes of wild horses with streaming tails and manes. Not a sign of vegetation was to be seen on that barren coast, nor any trace of human existence, save here a lonely house on the ridge, and yonder a dismantled wreck careened high upon the beach, or the ribs of some half-buried hulk protruding from the sand.

On the other side was an unbroken horizon of water. Numerous vessels of the fleet were still in sight. And now a little steamer came dashing gayly along, hailed with cheers. It was the Picket, General Burnside's flag-ship.

In the afternoon, more fog. But at sunset it was clear. The wind was light, blowing from the south. But now the ocean rolled in long, enormous swells, showing that the vessels were approaching Cape Hatteras; for, whatever may be the aspect of the sea elsewhere, here its billows are never at rest.

So the sun went down, and the night came on, with

its cold moon and stars, and Hatteras lighthouse shot its arrowy ray far out across the dark water.

The breeze freshened and increased to a gale; and the violence of the waves increased with it, until the schooner creaked and groaned in every part, and it seemed as if she must break in pieces. Sometimes the billows burst upon the deck with a thunder-crash, and, sweeping over it, poured in cataracts from her sides. Now a heavy cross-sea struck her beams with the jarring force of an avalanche of rocks, flinging more than one unlucky fellow clear from his berth. And now her bows went under, sunk by a weight of rolling water, from which it seemed for an instant impossible that she could ever emerge. But rise she did, each time, slowly, laboring, quivering, and groaning, like a living thing in mortal agony. Once, as she plunged, the great cable that united her fortunes with those of the steamer, unable to bear the tremendous strain, snapped like a wet string; and immediately she fell off helplessly before the gale.

The troops had a terrible night of it. Many were deathly sick. Two or three broke their watches, besides getting badly bruised, by pitching from their bunks. Frank would not have dared to go to sleep, even if he could. Once, when the ship gave a lurch, and stopped suddenly, striking the shoulder of a wave, he heard somebody tumble.

"Who's that?" he asked.

And the nasal sing-song of the poetical Tucket answered, "'Awaking with a start, the waters heave around me, and on high the winds lift up their voices; I depart, whither I know not; but the hour's gone by when Boston's lessening shores can grieve or glad mine eye.'"

And Tucket crept back into his bunk.

"We're all going to the bottom, I'm sure," whined John Winch, from the top berth, over Frank. "I believe we're sinking now."

"Well," said Frank, "the water will reach me first, and you'll be one of the last to go under; you've that for a satisfaction."

"I believe that's what he chose the top berth for," said Harris.

"How can you be joking, such a time as this?" said John. "Here's Atwater, fast asleep! Are you, Atwater?"

"No," said the soldier, who lay sick, with his thoughts far away.

"Ellis is; ain't you, Ellis?" And Jack reached to shake his comrade. "How can you be asleep, Ned, when we're all going to the bottom?"

"Let me alone!" growled Ned.

"We are going to the bottom," said Jack, — the ship just then rolling in the trough of the sea.

"I can't help it if we are," replied Ellis, sick and stupefied; "and I don't care much. Let me go to the bottom in peace."

"O Lord! O Lord! O Lord!" moaned Jack, in despair, feeling more like praying than ever before in his life.

Tucket had a line of poetry to suit his case: —

"'And then some prayed — the first time in some years;'" he said, quoting Byron. And he proceeded with a description of a shipwreck, which was not very edifying to the unhappy Winch: "'Then rose from sea to sky the wild farewell,'" &c.

"I never would have enlisted if I was such a coward as Jack," said Harris, contemptuously.

"I ain't a coward," retorted Jack. "I enlisted to fight, not to go to sea and be drownded."

"Drownded — ded — ded — dead!" said Tucket.

"O, yes," said Harris, "you are mighty fierce for getting ashore and fighting. But when you were on land you were just as glad to get to sea. Now I hope you'll get enough of it. I wouldn't mind a shipwreck myself, just to hear you scream."

Then Tucket: "'At first one universal shriek there rushed, louder than the loud ocean, — like a crash of echoing thunder; and then all was hushed, save the wild wind, and the remorseless dash of billows; but at intervals there gushed, accompanied with a convulsive splash, a solitary shriek — the bubbling cry of private Winch, in his last agony!'"

After this, conversation ceased for a time, and there was no noise but of the storm, and the groanings of the ship and of the sick.

Frank could not sleep, but, clinging to his berth, and listening to the shock of billows, thought of the other vessels of that brave fleet, scattered and tossed, and wondered at the awful power of the sea.

Then he remembered the story Corporal Gray had that day told them of the great Spanish Armada, which sailed in the days of Queen Elizabeth to invade England, and was blown to its destruction by the storms of the Almighty; and he questioned within himself whether this proud expedition was destined for a similar fate. Already he seemed to hear the lamentations of those at home, and the frantic rejoicings of the rebels.

The next morning the wind lulled; but the sea still ran high. The sun rose upon a scene of awful grandeur. The schooner was sailing under the few rags of canvas which had withstood the gale. The steamer was nowhere in sight; but other vessels of the shattered fleet could be seen, some near, and some half below the horizon, far out at sea. The waves, white-capped, green-streaked, ceaselessly shifting, with dark blue hollows and high-curved crests all bursting into foam, came chasing each other, and passed on like sliding liquid hills, spurning the schooner from their slippery backs.

"'Roll on, thou deep and dark blue ocean! roll! ten thousand fleets sweep over thee in vain!'" observed Tucket, coming on deck with Frank, and gazing around at the few tossed remnants of the storm-scattered expedition.

Wild and terribly beautiful the scene was; and Frank, who had often wished to behold the ocean in its fury, was now sufficiently recovered from his sickness to enjoy the opportunity. Nor was the wondering delight with which he saw the sun rise out of the deep, and shine across the tumbling yeasty waves, at all diminished by the drolleries of his friend Seth, who kept at his side, saying the queerest things, and ever and anon shouting poetry to the running seas.

"'Though the strained mast should quiver as a reed, and the rent canvas fluttering strew the gale, still must I on; for I am as a weed flung from the rocks on Ocean's foam to sail, where'er secession breeds, or treason's works prevail,'"—added Seth, altering the verse to suit the occasion.

The fleet had indeed been rudely handled in that rough night off the cape. But now sail after sail hove in sight, all making their way as best they could towards the inlet. This some reached, and got safely in before night. Others, attempting to enter, got aground, and were with difficulty got off again. Some anchored outside, and some lay off and on, waiting for morning, to be piloted past the shoals, and through the narrow channel, to a safe anchorage inside.

XV.

HATTERAS INLET.

BUT what a morning dawned! Another storm, more terrible than the first, had been raging all night, and its violence was still increasing. And now it came on to rain; and rain and wind and sea appeared to vie with each other in wreaking their fury on the ill-starred expedition.

Tuesday night the storm abated, and Wednesday brought fair weather. The fleet in the mean time had suffered perils and hardships which can never be told. Many of the transports were still missing. Many were at anchor outside the inlet, waiting for pilots to bring them in. Some had been lost. The " City of New York," a large steam propeller, freighted with stores and munitions of war, had struck on the bar, and foundered in the breakers. The crew, after clinging for twenty-four hours in the rigging to avoid being washed off by the sea, which made a clean breach over her, had been saved, but vessel and cargo were a total loss. Frank had watched the wreck, which seemed at one moment to emerge from the waves, and the next was half hidden by the incoming billows, and enveloped in a white shroud of foam.

The schooner had escaped the dangers of the sea, and was safe at last inside the inlet; as safe, at least, as any of the fleet, in so precarious an anchorage.

There was still another formidable bar to pass before the open waters of Pamlico Sound could be entered. The transports that had got in were lying in a basin, full of shoals, with but little room to swing with the tide, and they were continually running into each other, or getting aground. Nor was it encouraging to see bales of hay from one of the wrecks lodge at low water upon the very sand-bar which the fleet had still to cross.

Frank and his comrades took advantage of the fair weather to make observations of the two forts, Hatteras and Clark, which command the situation. These were constructed by the rebels, but had been captured from them by General Butler and Commodore Stringham, in August, 1861, and were now garrisoned by national troops. They stand on the south-western limb of one of the low, barren islands which separate this part of Pamlico Sound from the Atlantic. Between two narrow sand-spits the tides rush in and out with great force and rapidity; and this is the inlet —

a mere passage cut through into the sound by the action of the sea.

As the schooner was being towed farther in, some men in a boat, who had been ashore at Fort Hatteras, and were returning to their ship, came alongside. The party consisted of some officers belonging to a New Jersey regiment, together with a boat's crew of six men.

"Throw us a line," they said; "and tow us along."

A line was flung to them from the schooner; but they had some difficulty in getting it, for the waves were running high in the channel. Pending the effort, the tiller slipped from the hands of the officer who was steering; a heavy sea struck the boat on the quarter, and she capsized. Boats were lowered from the schooner, and sent to the rescue. It was a scene of intense and anxious interest to Frank, who was on deck and saw it all. The men in the water righted the boat several times, but she filled and capsized as often. One officer was seen to get his feet entangled, sink with his head downward, and drown in that position before he could be extricated. He was the colonel of the regiment. The surgeon of the regiment also perished. All the rest were saved.

The drowned bodies were brought upon deck, and every effort was made to bring back life into them; but in vain. And there they lay; so full of hope, and courage, and throbbing human life an hour ago — now two pale, livid corpses. The incident made a strong impression on Frank, not yet accustomed to the aspect of death, which was destined to become so familiar to his eyes a few days later.

Still the dangers and delays that threatened to prove fatal to the expedition were far from ended. It seemed that the rebels were the enemies it had least to fear. Avarice, incapacity, and treachery at home had conspired with the elements against it. Many of the larger vessels drew too much water for the passage into the sound, and were wholly unfit for the voyage.

" The contractors," said Burnside, " have ruined me; but God holds me in his palm, and all will yet be well."

With nothing to distinguish him but his yellow belt, in blue shirt, slouched hat, and high boots, he stood like a sea god (says an eye-witness) in the bows of his light boat, speaking every vessel, and inquiring affectionately about the welfare of the men.

Storm succeeded storm, while the fleet was yet at the inlet; many days elapsing before the principal vessels could be got over the " bulkhead," as the bar is called, which still intervened between them and the sound. To add to the sufferings of the troops, the supply of fresh water gave out. Much of that with

11

demon of thirst at bay until the water vessels could arrive.

Ten days elapsed after the schooner entered the inlet before she was got over the bulkhead into the open sound. And still ten days more were destined to slip by before any general movement against the enemy was attempted by the fleet. In the mean while the troops confined on shipboard resorted to a thousand devices for passing away the time. There was dancing, there was card-playing, there was singing; and many new games were invented for the occasion. Frank learned the manual of arms.

Something else he learned, not so much to his credit. Before saying what that was, I wish to remind the reader of the peculiar circumstances in which he was placed — the tedious hours; the hardships, which he was glad to forget at any cost; the example of companions, all older, and many so much older than himself; and, not least by any means, his own ardent and susceptible nature.

One day he joined his comrades in a game of bluff. Now, bluff is a game there is no fun in unless some stake is played for. The boys had been ashore, and gathered some pebbles and shells from the beach, and these were used for the purpose. Frank had great success. He won more shells than any body. In the excitement, he forgot his thirst, and all the accompa-

nying troubles. He forgot, too, that this was a kind of gambling. And he was so elated, that when somebody proposed to play for pennies, he did not think that it would be much worse to do that than to play for shells and pebbles.

Unfortunately, he was still successful. He won twenty cents in about an hour. He did not intend to keep them, for he did not think that would be right. "I'll play," said he, "and let the boys win them back again." But, at the next sitting, he won still more pennies; so that he thought he could well afford to play a bolder game. His success was all the more gratifying when he considered that he was the youngest of the party, and that by skill and good fortune he was beating his elders.

One day, after he had won more than a dollar, — which seems a good deal of money to a boy in his condition, — he began to lose. This was not so amusing. He had made up his mind that when his winnings were gone, he would stop playing; and the idea of stopping was not pleasant to contemplate. How could he give up a sport which surpassed every thing else in the way of excitement? However, he determined to keep his resolution. And it was soon brought to a test.

The luck had turned, and Frank found himself where he began. If he played any more, he must risk his own money. He didn't mind losing a few pennies, — that was nothing serious; but the boys were not playing for simple pennies now.

"I believe I've played enough, boys," said he, passing his hand across his heated brow, and casting his eyes around at objects which looked strange to them after their long and intense application to the cards.

"O, of course!" sneered Jack Winch, who was watching the game, "Frank 'll stop as soon as he is beginning to lose a little."

Jack was not playing, for a very good reason. He had spent nearly all his money, and lost the rest. He had lost some of it to Frank, and was consequently very desirous of seeing the latter brought to the same condition as himself.

The sneering remark stung Frank. He would gladly have pleaded Jack's excuse for not playing any more; but he had still in his pocket over two dollars of the money he had reserved for himself when the troops were paid off. And it did seem rather mean in him, now he thought of it, to throw up the game the moment others were serving him as he had been only too willing to serve them.

"I'm not afraid of losing my money," said he, blushing; "but I've had enough play for one day."

"You didn't get sick of it so easy when the luck

was on your side," said Harris, who had lost money to Frank, and now wanted his revenge.

"For instance, yesterday, when the Parrott was talking to the boy," said Seth.

The Parrott he spoke of was one of the twelve-pound Parrott guns the schooner carried; and the boy was the *buoy*, or target, in the water, at which the gunners had practised firing round shot. Frank remembered how all wanted to put aside the cards and watch the sport except himself. At another time he would have taken great interest in it, and have been on hand to cheer as enthusiastically as any body when the well-aimed shots struck the water; but his mind was completely absorbed in winning money. There was no such noble diversion on deck to-day; and it was only too easy to see his real reason for getting so soon tired of bluff.

"That's right, Frank; stop! Now's a good time," said Atwater, who watched the game a good deal, but never took a hand in it.

"Well, I shan't urge him, ef he's in 'arnest," said Seth; "though he has kep' me at it a darned sight longer 'n I wanted to, sometimes, when 'twas my tin 'stid of his'n that was goin' by the board. Stop where ye be, my bold drummer boy; keep yer money, ef ye've got any left; that is the best way, after all. 'I know the right, and I approve it, too; I know the wrong, and yet the wrong pursue,'" added Tucket, dealing the cards.

No doubt he meant to give Frank good advice. But to the sensitive and proud spirit of the boy, it sounded like withering sarcasm. He couldn't stand that.

"I'll play fifteen minutes longer," said he, looking at his watch, "if that'll please you.'

"A quarter of an hour!" said Harris, contemptuously. "We'd better all stop now, and come at it fresh again, by and by."

The proposition was acceded to; for what could Frank say against it? He had not the courage to say, "Boys, I feel that I have been doing wrong, and I mean to stop at once;" but he thought it more manly to play once more, if only to show that he was not afraid of losing. "And perhaps," he thought, remembering his former luck, "I shall win."

XVI.

HOW FRANK LOST HIS WATCH.

PLAY again he did accordingly; and, sure enough, he won. He brought Tucket to his last dime. The poetical and philosophic spirit in which that good-humored young man contemplated his losses, was worthy of a better cause.

"'Fare thee well, and, ef forever, still forever fare thee well,'" he remarked, staking the said dime. And when it was lost,—for Frank "raked the pile,"—he added, pathetically, going from Byron to Burns, "'Fare thee weel, thou brightest, fairest; fare thee weel, thou last and dearest! Had we never loved sae kindly, had we never loved sae blindly, never met, or never parted, I had ne'er been broken-hearted.' Boys, I'm dead broke, and must quit off, without some of you that are flush will lend me a quarter."

"Ask Frank," said Ellis; "he's the flushest."

So Frank lent Seth a quarter, and with that quarter Seth won back all his money, and, in the course of two more sittings, cleaned Frank out, as the phrase is

Then, one would say, Frank had a valid excuse to
retire, if not before. He had risked his money, and
lost it. Certainly nothing more could be expected
of him. Seth grinned, and Jack Winch rubbed his
hands with delight.

But now *Frank* was not content. His heart was
gnawed by chagrin. He had not really wished to
stop playing at all; for the sense of vacancy and
craving which always, in such natures, succeeds the
cessation of unhealthy excitement, is misery enough in
itself. But to have left off with as much money in his
pocket as he began with, would have been felicity,
compared with the bitter consciousness of folly, the
stinging vexation and regret, which came with his
misfortunes.

"I'll lend ye, if ye like," said the good-natured
Seth — perhaps in return for the similar favor he had
received; or rather because he pitied the boy, and
meant to let him win back his money; for, with all
his mischief and drollery, this Tucket was one of the
most generous and kind-hearted of Frank's friends.

The offer was gladly accepted; and Frank, praying
Fortune to favor him, made a promise in his heart,
that, if she would aid him to recover his losses, he
would then bid farewell forever to the enticing
game.

But the capricious goddess does not answer prayers.

On the contrary, she delights to side with those who need her least, spurning away the supplicants at her feet.

Frank borrowed a quarter, and lost it immediately. He borrowed again, determined to play more carefully. He waited until he had an excellent hand, then staked his money.

Tucket and Ellis did not play; and the game was between Frank and Harris. Both were confident, and they kept doubling their stakes, Frank borrowing again and again of Seth for the purpose. He held four kings, the strongest hand but one in the game. He knew Harris's style of playing too well to be much daunted by his audacity, not believing that he held that one stronger hand than his.

"I'll lend ye as long as ye call for more," said Seth; "only, seeing you've borrowed already more'n I've won of ye, s'posin' ye give me some security?"

"I've nothing to give," said Frank.

"There's your watch," suggested Winch, who had had a glimpse of Joe's cards. And at the same time he winked significantly, giving Frank to understand that his antagonist had not a hand of very great strength.

Thus encouraged, sure of victory, and too much beside himself to consider the sacred nature of the object he was placing in pawn, Frank handed over his watch to Seth, and received from him loan after loan, until he was eight dollars in his debt. Seth did not like to advance any more than that on the watch. So the critical moment arrived. Frank, with flushed face and trembling hands, placed his all upon the board. Then Harris, showing his cards with a smile, swept the pile towards his cap.

"Let me see!" cried Frank, incredulous, staying his arm until he could be sure of the cards.

His flushed face turned white; his hand fell upon the bench as if suddenly palsied.

"Two pairs of aces! that's what I call luck, Joe," said Winch, scarce able to restrain his joyous chuckling.

Frank looked up at him with wild distress and kindling fury in his face.

"It was you, Jack Winch! You made me——"

"Made you what?" said John, insolently.

What, indeed? He had by looks, which spoke as plainly as words, assured Frank that Harris held but an indifferent hand; whereas he held the best the pack afforded. By that falsehood,—for, with looks and actions at your command, it is not necessary to open your mouth in order to tell the most downright, absolute lie.—he had induced Frank to play on boldly to his own ruin.

But was he alone to blame? Even if he had told

the truth about Joe's hand, ought Frank to have been influenced by it? He had no right to that knowledge, and to take advantage of it was dishonest.

No doubt Frank himself thought so, now he reflected upon it. To accuse Jack was to confess his own disingenuousness. He was by nature as fair and open as the day; he despised a base deception; and it was only as an inevitable consequence of such wrong doings as lead directly to faithlessness and duplicity, that he could ever become guilty of these immoralities.

Such is the vice of gambling — a process by which men hope to obtain their neighbors' goods without yielding an equivalent for them; and which, therefore, inflames covetousness, and accustoms the mind to the contemplation of unjust gains, until it is ready to resort to any unjust means of securing them. Do you say there are honest gamblers? The term is a contradiction. You might, with equal consistency, talk of truthful liars. To get your money, or any thing else, without rendering an equitable return, is the core of all dishonesty, whether in the gamester, the pickpocket, the man who cheats in trade, or the boy who robs orchards. And a conscience once debauched by dishonest aims, will not, as I said, long scruple at unfair means.

Singularly enough, Frank was more abashed by the betrayal of the unfair means he had attempted to use, than he had yet been by any consciousness of the immorality of the practice which led to them. He could not say to Winch, "You told me I was sure of winning, and so deceived me." He only looked at him a moment, with wild distress and exasperation on his face, which quickly changed to ·an expression of morose and bitter despair; and dropping his head, and putting up his hands, he burst into irrepressible sobs.

"My watch! my watch that was given to me —" and which he had so ignominiously gambled away. No wonder he wept. No wonder he shook from head to foot with the passion of grief, as the conviction of his own folly and infatuation burned like intolerable fire in his soul.

"Dry up, baby!" said Jack, through his teeth. "There comes the captain."

Baby? Poor Frank! It was because he was not altogether given over to recklessness and vice that he cried at the thought of his lost watch, and of his gross ingratitude to the unknown giver. Still he felt that it was weak in him to cry. He who risks his property in order to get possession of another's should be philosopher enough to take with equanimity the loss of his own.

"Don't be childish, Frank; don't be silly!" said his friends.

And, indeed, he had the strongest reason for suppressing his sobs. Captain Edney was approaching. He was the last person to whom he would have wished to betray his guilt and misfortune. He loved and respected him; and we fear most the disapprobation of those we love and respect. Moreover, through him the heart-breaking intelligence of her son's evil courses might reach Mrs. Manly. But no doubt Frank's chief motive for concealing the cause of his grief from Captain Edney was the suspicion he still entertained, notwithstanding that officer's professed ignorance of the entire matter, that he was in reality the secret donor of the watch. So he choked back his sobs, and pretended to be assorting some pebbles, which the boys used as counters, especially when certain officers were passing, who would have reproved them if they had seen money on the board. And Captain Edney, whether he suspected any thing wrong, or not, walked on; and that restraint upon Frank's feelings was removed.

But having once controlled the outburst, he did not suffer them to get the better of him again. With a look of silent and sullen despair, he got up, and went to his bunk, and threw himself upon it, and, turning his face to the wall, refused to be comforted.

It was the wooden wall of the ship's timbers — the same he had looked at in sickness, in storms at sea, by day, and at night by the dim light of the swinging ship's lanterns; and when he lay calmly at rest, in the palm of God, amid the convulsions and dangers of the deep, and when, in the tediousness of long, dull days of waiting, he had lain there, and solaced himself with sweet thoughts of home.

But never had the ribbed ship's side appeared to him as now. And yet it was the same; but he was not the same. He was no longer the bright, hopeful, happy boy as before, but miserable, guilty, broken-hearted. And as we are, so is the world to us; the most familiar objects changing their aspect with every change in the soul. Does the sunshine, which was bright yesterday, look cold to-day? and is the sweet singing of birds suddenly become as a mockery to the ear? and the faces of friends, late so pleasant to see, have they grown strange and reproachful? and is life, before so full of hope, turned sour, and vapid, and bitter? O, my friend, I pity you; but the change, which you probably think is in the world, is only in yourself.

"The parson seems to have fallen from grace," said John Winch, sarcastically.

"Hold your tongue!" said Atwater, sternly. "You are all more to blame than he is. Of course, a boy of his age will do what he sees older ones do. It's a shame to get his money and watch away from him so."

And the honest fellow went and sat by Frank, and tried to console him.

"Go away! go away!" said Frank, in his anguish. "Don't trouble yourself about such a miserable fool as I am. I deserve it all. Let me be!"

Atwater, who was sadly deficient in what is called the gift of gab, had no soothing words at his command, full as his heart was of compassion. And after sitting some time by the unhappy boy, patting him softly on the shoulder, he arose, and went away; concluding that his absence would be a relief to one so utterly miserable.

Then Seth Tucket came, and took his place.

"That's always the way with bad luck, I swan," he said, sympathizingly. "Misfortunes always come in heaps. It never rains but it pours."

"I wish you'd let me alone!" said the boy, peevishly.

"That's fair, I swan!" said Seth. "But le' me tell ye. Ef I hed won the watch, I'd give it back to ye in a minute. But Harris is the winner, and I've only the watch now to show for my money. But here's a half dollar to begin again with. You know what luck is at cards, — how it shifts, now this way, now that, like a cow's tail in fly-time, — and I hain't the least doubt but with that half dollar you'll win back all your money, and your watch too."

The offer was kindly meant; and it encouraged a little spark of comfort in Frank's heart. To win back his losses — that was his only hope. He took the money, silently pressing Seth's hand. After that he struggled to forget his grief in thoughts of his former good fortune, which he believed would now return to him.

12

XVII.

IN WHICH FRANK SEES STRANGE THINGS.

In this frame of mind, Frank went on deck. He saw the old drum-major coming towards him. Being in any thing but a social mood, he tried to avoid him; and turning his back, walked away. But the veteran followed, and came to his side.

"Well, my young man," said the old cynic, exhibiting a little agitation, and speaking in a hurried tone, unusual with him, "I hear brave tidings of you."

His voice sounded harsh and sarcastic to the irritated boy; and, indeed, there was resentment enough in the veteran's breast, as well as a bitter sense of injury and disappointment, as he spoke.

Frank, nursing his sore heart, the wounds of which he could not bear to have touched by the most friendly hand, compressed his lips together, and made no reply.

"So you have been really gambling — have you?" added the old man, in tones of suppressed emotion.

"That's my business," said Frank, curtly.

He regretted the undutiful words the instant they escaped his lips. But he was too proud to ask pardon for them. As for the old man, he stood silent for a long time, looking down at the boy, who looked not up again at him. And there was a tremor in his lip, and a dilatation in his eye, which at length grew misty with a tear that gathered, but did not fall. And with a sigh, he turned away.

"Well, be it so!" Frank heard him say, as if to himself. "I thought — I hoped — but no matter."

He thought — he hoped — what? That his early faith in love and friendship, which had so long been dead, might be raised to life again by this boy, for whom he had conceived so singular a liking, and who, like all the rest, proved ungrateful and unworthy when the hour of trial came.

Alas! such is the result of our transgressions. Once having offended our own souls, we are quick to offend others. And vice makes us irritable, ungenerous, unjust. And not a crime can be committed, but its evil consequences follow, not the author of it only, but also the innocent, upon whom its blighting shadow falls.

"Frank, if you want some fun!" said an eager whisper, with a promise of mischief in it; a hand at the same time twitching the boy's coat.

It was Ned Ellis, who had come for him, and was

hastening away again. Frank followed — all too
ready for any enterprise that would bring the balm
of forgetfulness to his hurt mind.

The boys entered the hold of the vessel, where, in
the hush and obscurity, a group of their companions
stood or sat, among the barrels and boxes, still as
statues, until they recognized the new comers.

"All right! nobody but us," whispered Ned, clam-
bering over the freight, accompanied by Frank.

"Come along, and make no noise, if you value your
hides," said Harris. "Here, Frank, is something to
console ye for your bad luck." And he held out
something in a tin cup.

"What is it?" said Frank; "water?"

"Something almost as good," said Harris. "It was
water the boys came down here in search of; and
they've tapped five barrels of sirup in the operation,
and finally they've stuck the gimlet into a cask of —
taste on't."

Frank knew what it was by the smell. It was not
the first time he had smelt whiskey; or tasted it,
either. But hitherto he had stopped at the taste,
having nothing but his curiosity to gratify. Now,
however, he had something else to gratify — a burning
thirst of the body, aggravated by his feverish excitement, and a burning thirst of the soul, which de-

manded stimulus of any kind whatsoever that would allay the inward torment.

And so he drank. He did not love the liquor, although the rank taste of it was ameliorated by a liberal admixture of sirup. But he felt the internal sinking and wretchedness of heart and stomach braced up and assuaged by the first draught; so he took another. And for the same reason he indulged in a third. And so it happened that his head began shortly to swim, his eyes to see double, and things to look queer to them generally. The dim hold of the vessel might have been the pit of darkness, and the obscure grinning faces of his comrades might have been those of imps therein abiding, for aught he knew to the contrary, or cared. He began to laugh.

" What's the matter, Frank ? "

" Nothing," he said, thickly; " only it's so droll." And he sat down on a cask, laughing again with uncontrollable merriment — at nothing; an infallible symptom that a person is either tipsy or a fool. But Frank was not a fool. *Ergo :* he was tipsy.

" Get him up as quick as we can, boys," he heard some one saying, " or else we can't get him up at all."

" Better leave him here till he gets over it," said another. " That 'll be the best way."

" Who'd have thought a little dodger like that

would upset him?" said somebody else. "By George, we'll all get found out, through him."

"Whads mare?" said Frank, meaning to ask, "What is the matter?" but somehow he could not make his organs of articulation go off right. "'Zis wachecall drung?" (Is this what you call drunk?)

"Can ye walk?" — He recognized the voice of his friend Tucket. — "It's too bad to leave him here, boys. We must get him to his berth 'fore he's any worse."

"Zhue, Sef?" (Is it you, Seth?) Frank, with the help of his friend, got upon his feet. "No, I don' breeve I'm drung; I be bernaliddlewile;" meaning to say he did not believe he was intoxicated, and to express his conviction that he would be better in a little while.

Seth repeated his first inquiry.

"Izzindee! I kung wong!" (Yes, indeed, I can walk.) And Frank, as if to demonstrate the absurdity of the pretence, went stumbling loosely over the freight, saved from falling only by the assistance of his friend.

"Here's the ladder," said Tucket; "now be careful."

"'M I goung upthlarer, or 'm I goung downthlarer?" (Was he going up the ladder, or was he going down the ladder?)

Tucket proceeded to show him that the ladder was to be ascended; and, directing him how to hold on, and how to place his feet, boosted him gently, while a comrade above drew him also gently, until he was got safely out.

"I did that perrywell!" said Frank. "Now lemmehell Sef!" (Now let me help Seth.) "You're a bully fellel, Sef. I'll hellup ye!"

"Thank ye, boy," said Tucket; indulging him in the ludicrous notion that *he* was helping *his friends*. "Much obliged."

"Nod tall!" (Not at all,) said Frank. "Bully fellels like youme mushellpitchuthth." (Must help each other.) "You unstan me, Sef?"

"Yes, I understand you. But keep quiet now, and come along with me."

So saying, the athletic soldier threw his arm affectionately around Frank, hurried him away to his bunk, and tumbled him into it without much ceremony.

Not unobserved, however. Captain Edney, who had had an anxious eye on Frank of late, saw him retire to his quarters in this rather suspicious manner.

"What's the matter with him?" he inquired of Seth.

"Nothing very serious, I believe, sir," replied

Tucket, with the most perfect seriousness. "A little seasick, or sunthin of the kind. He'll git over it in a jiffy."

The waves were not running sufficiently high in the sound, however, to render the theory of seasickness very plausible; and, to satisfy his mind, Captain Edney approached Frank's bunk, putting to him the same question.

Frank replied in scarcely intelligible language, with a swimming gaze, tending to the cross-eyed, at the captain, "that there was nothing in partiggler the mare with him, but he was very busy.

"Busy?" said Captain Edney, severely; "what do you mean?"

"Not busy; but *busy, busy!*" repeated Frank.

"You mean dizzy?"

"Yes, thad's it! bizzy." He had somehow got *boozy* and *dizzy* mixed up.

"What makes you dizzy?"

"Boys gimme some drink, I donowat."

"The boys gave you some drink? You don't know what? — Tucket," said Captain Edney, "what's all this? Who has been getting that boy drunk?"

Seth perceived that any attempt to disguise the truth would be futile, except so far as it might be possible by ingenious subtleties to shield his companions. The alarm, he believed, must have reached them by this time, and have scattered the group at the whiskey barrel; so he answered boldly, —

"The fact, sir, is jest this. We've been about half crazy for water, as you know, for the past week or two; and men'll do almost any thing for relief, under such circumstances. It got rumored around, somehow, that there was plenty of water in the vessel, and the boys went to hunting for't, and stumbled on the quartermaster's stores, and tapped a few casks, I believe, mostly sirup, but one turned out to be whiskey. Dry as we be, it's no more'n nat'ral 't we should drink a drop, under the circumstances."

"Who tapped the casks?"

"That's more 'n I know. I didn't see it done," said Seth.

"Who drank?"

"I drinked a little, for one; jest enough to know 't wan't water."

"And how many of you are drunk?" demanded Captain Edney.

"I a'n't, for one. But I believe Manly is a little how-come-ye-so. I'll say this for him, though: he had nothing to do with tapping the casks, and he didn't seem to know what it was the boys gin him. He was dry; it tasted sweet, and he drinked, nat'rally."

"Who gave him the whiskey?"

" I didn't notice, particularly," said Seth.

His accomplices were summoned, the quartermaster was notified, and the affair was still further investigated. All confessed to having tasted the liquor, but nobody knew who tapped the casks, or who had given the whiskey to Frank, and all had the same plausible excuse for their offence — intolerable thirst. It was impossible, where all were leagued together, and all seemed equally culpable, to single out the ringleaders for punishment, and it was not desirable to punish all. After a while, therefore, the men were dismissed with a reprimand, and the subject postponed indefinitely. That very afternoon forty barrels of water came on board, and the men had no longer a pretext for tapping casks in the hold; and a few days later was the battle, in which they wiped out by their bravery all memory of past transgressions.

And Frank? The muss, as the boys called it, was over before his senses recovered from their infinite bewilderment. He lay stupefied in his bunk, which went whirling round and round with him, sinking down and down and down, into void and bottomless chaos, where solid earth was none — type of the drunkard's moral state, where virtue has lost its foot-hold, and there is no firm ground of self-respect, and conscience is a loosened ledge toppling treacherously, and there is no steady hope to stay his

horrible whirling and sinking. Stupefaction became
sleep; with sleep inebriation passed; and Frank
awoke to misery.

It was evening. The boys were playing cards
again by the light of the ship's lantern. The noise
and the glimmer reached Frank in his berth, and
called him back to time and space and memory. He
remembered his watch, his insolent reply to his old
friend Sinjin, the scene in the hold of the vessel, the
sweet-tasting stuff, and the dizziness, a strange ladder
somewhere which he had either climbed or dreamed of
climbing; and he thought of his mother and sisters
with a pang like the sting of a scorpion. He could
bear any thing but that.

He got up, determined not to let vain regrets torment him. He shut out from his mind those pure
images of home, the presence of which was maddening
to him. Having stepped so deep into guilt, he would
not, he could not, turn back. For Frank carried even
into his vices that steadiness of resolution which dis-
tinguishes such natures from those of the Jack Winch
stamp, wavering and fickle alike in good and ill. He
possessed that perseverance and purpose which go to
form either the best and noblest men, or, turned to
evil, the most hardy and efficient villains. Frank was
no milksop.

"O, I'm all right," said he, with a reckless laugh, in

reply to his comrades' bantering. "Give me a chance there — can't you?"

For he was bent on winning back his watch. It seemed that nothing short of the impossible could turn him aside from that intent. The players made room for him, and he prepared his counters, and took up his cards.

"What do you do, Frank?" was asked impatiently; all were waiting for him.

What ailed the boy? He held his cards, but he was not looking at them. His eyes were not on the board, nor on his companions, nor on any object there. But he was staring with a pallid, intense expression — at something. There were anguish, and alarm, and yearning affection in his look. His hair was disordered, his countenance was white and amazed; his comrades were astonished as they watched him.

"What's the matter, Frank? what's the matter?"

Their importunity brought him to himself.

"Did you see?" he asked in a whisper.

They had seen nothing that he had seen. Then it was all an illusion? a fragment of his drunken dreams? But no drunken dream was ever like that.

"Yes, I'll play," he said, trying to collect himself; thinking that he would forget the illusion, and remembering he had his watch to win back.

But his heart failed him. His brain, his hand failed him also. Absolutely, he could not play.

"Boys, I'm not very well. Excuse me — I can't play to-night."

And hesitatingly, like a person who has been stunned, he got up, and left the place. Few felt inclined to jeer him. John Winch began to say something about "the parson going to pray," but it was frowned down.

Frank went on deck. The evening was mild, the wind was south, the sky was clear and starry; it was like a May night in New England. The schooner was riding at anchor in the sound; other vessels of the fleet lay around her, rocking gently on the tide — dim hulls, with glowing, fiery eyes; and here there was a band playing, and from afar off came the sound of solemn singing, wafted on the wind. And the water was all a weltering waste of waves and molten stars.

But little of all this Frank saw, or heard, or heeded. His soul was rapt from him; he was lost in wonder and grief.

"Can you tell me any thing?" said a voice at his side.

"O, Atwater," said Frank, clutching his hand, "what does it mean? As I was playing, I saw — I saw — every thing else disappeared; cards, count-

ers, the bench we were playing on, and there before
me, as plainly as I ever saw any thing in my life ——"

"What was it?" asked Atwater, as Frank paused,
unable to proceed.

"My sister Hattie," then said Frank, in a whisper
of awe, "in her coffin! in her shroud! But she did
not seem dead at all. She was white as the purest
snow; and she smiled up at me — such a sweet, sad
smile — O! O!"

And Frank wrung his hands.

XVIII.

BITTER THINGS.

ATWATER could not have said much to comfort him, even if he had had the opportunity. Some young fellows who had heard of Frank's losses at bluff, and of his intoxication, saw him on deck, and came crowding around to have some jokes with him. Atwater retired. And Frank, who had little relish for jokes just then, went below, and got into his berth, where he could be quiet, and think a little.

But thinking alone there with his conscience was torture to him. He turned on his bed, and looked, and saw Atwater sitting in his bunk, with a book in his hand, reading by the dim light. The card-playing was going on close by, and jokes and oaths and laughter were heard on all sides; but Atwater heeded no one, and no one heeded him.

Only Frank: he regarded the still, earnest soldier a long time, silently admiring his calmness and strength, so perfectly expressed in his mild, firm, kindly, taciturn face, and wondering what book he had.

"What are you reading, Atwater?" he at length asked.

"My Bible," replied the soldier, giving him a grave, pleasant smile.

Frank felt pained, — almost jealous. I can't tell how it is, but we don't like too well the sight of our companions cheerfully performing those duties which we neglect or hate. Cain slew Abel for that cause.

"I didn't know you read that," said Frank.

"I never have too much. But my wife —— " The soldier's voice always sunk with a peculiarly tender thrill whenever he spoke of his bride of an hour, or rather of a minute, whom he had wedded and left in such haste. "She slipped a Bible in my knapsack unbeknown to me. I had a letter from her to-day, in which she asks me if I read it. So I must read it, and say yes, if only to please her. But the truth is," said Atwater, with a brightening eye, "I find good in it I never thought was there before."

Frank had no word to answer him. Conscience-stricken, sick at heart, miserable as he could be, he could only lie there in his berth, and look at the brave soldier, and envy him.

He remembered how, not long ago, when his mother's wishes were more to him than they had been of late, he had desired to read his Testament for her sake, but had not dared to do so openly, fearing the sneers of his comrades. And his mother, in every letter, repeated her injunction, "My son, read your Testament;"—which had become to him as the idle wind. For never now, either by stealth or openly, did he read that book.

Yet here was this plain, honest soldier,—many called him dull,—for whom a word from one he loved was sufficient; he took the book as if that word were law. And the looks, the jests, which Frank had feared, were nothing to him.

Ashamed, remorseful, angry with himself, the boy lay thinking what he should do. A few bitter moments only. Then, opening his knapsack, he took out his Testament, and sitting in his bunk so that the light would shine on the page, opened it and read. His companions saw, and were surprised enough. But nobody jeered. What was the reason, I wonder?

And this was what Frank read. Written on a blank leaf, with a pencil, in his own hand, were these words:—

"*I do now solemnly promise my mother and sisters that, when I am in the army, I will never be guilty of swearing, or gambling, or drinking, or any other mean thing I know they would not approve of. And I do solemnly pledge my word that they shall sooner hear of my death than of my being guilty of any of those things.* FRANK MANLY."

13

And beneath those words were written these also, in his mother's hand : —

"*O heavenly Father! I beseech Thee, help my dear son to keep his promises. Give him strength to resist temptation. Save him, I pray Thee, from those who kill the body, but above all from those who kill the soul. If it be Thy gracious will, let him pass safely through whatever evils may beset him, and return to us uncontaminated and unhurt. But if this may not be, then, O, our Saviour! take him, take my precious child, I implore Thee, pure unto Thyself. And help us all so to live, that we shall meet again in joy and peace, if not here, hereafter. Amen.*"

Frank did not turn that page, but sat looking at it long. And he saw something besides the words there written. He saw himself once more a boy at home, the evening before his enlistment; pencil in hand, writing that solemn promise ; his mother watching near; the bright face of his sister Helen yonder, shadowed by the thought of his going; the little invalid Hattie on the lounge, her sad face smiling very much as he saw it smiling out just now from the flowers in the coffin.

He saw his mother also, pencil in hand, writing that prayer, — her countenance full of anxious love and tears, her gentle lips tremulous with blessings. He saw her come to his bed in the moonlight night, when last he slept there with little Willie at his side, as maybe he will never sleep again. And he heard her counsels and entreaties, as she knelt there beside him; and felt her kisses; and lived over once more the thoughts of that night after she was gone, and when he lay sleepless with the moonlight on his bed.

But here he was now — not away there in the room at home, but here, among soldiers, on shipboard. And the pure, innocent Frank of that night lived no more. And all those promises had been broken, one by one. And he knew not what to do, he was so miserable.

Yet — the sudden thought warmed and thrilled his breast — he might be pure as then, he might be innocent as then, and all the stronger for having known what temptation was, and fallen, and risen again. And he might keep those promises in a higher and nobler sense than he dreamed of when he made them; and his mother's prayer might, after all, be answered.

"Frank," said the voice of Captain Edney. He had come to visit the quarters of his company, and, seeing the boy sitting there so absorbed, his young face charged with thought and grief, had stopped some moments to regard him, without speaking.

Frank started, almost like a guilty person, and gave the military salute rather awkwardly as he got upon his feet. He had been secretly dreading Captain Edney's displeasure, and now he thought he was to be called to an account.

"I have something for you in my room," said the officer, with a look of serious reserve, unlike the cheerful, open, brotherly glance with which he formerly regarded the drummer boy.

Frank accompanied him, wondering what that something was. A reproof for his drunkenness, or for gambling away the watch, he expected more than any thing else; and his heart was heavy by the way.

"Did you know a mail came on board to-day?" said the captain, as they entered his state-room.

Frank remembered hearing Atwater say he had that day got a letter from his wife. But his mind had been too much agitated by other things to consider the subject then.

"No, sir, I didn't know it."

"How happens that? You are generally one of the most eager to receive letters."

Frank hung his head. What answer could he make? That he was intoxicated in his berth when the mail arrived? A sweat of shame covered him. He was silent.

"Well, well, my boy!" — Captain Edney patted him gently on the shoulder, — "you are forgiven this time. I am sure you did not mean to get drunk."

"O, sir!" began Frank, but stopped there, over-whelmed by the captain's kindness.

"I know all about it," said Captain Edney. "Tuck-et assures me that he and the rest were more to blame than you. But, for the sake of your friends, Frank, take warning by this experience, and never be be-trayed into any thing of the kind again. I trust you. And here, my boy, are your letters."

He put half a dozen into Frank's hands. And Frank, as he took them, felt his very heart melt with-in him with gratitude and contrition. He was not thinking so much of the letters as of Captain Edney and his watch.

"Forgive me; forgive me!" he humbly entreated.

"I do, freely, as I told you," said the captain.

"But — the watch you gave me!"

"Dear boy!" — the captain put his arm kindly about him, — "haven't I always told you I knew nothing about the watch? I did not give it to you, nor do I know what generous friend did."

"It is true, then?" Frank looked up with a half-glad, half-disappointed expression. He was disap-pointed to know that so good a friend was not the donor of the watch, and yet glad that he had not wronged *him* by gambling it away. "Then, Captain Edney, I wish you would tell me what to do. I have done the worst and meanest thing. I have lost the watch."

And he went on to relate how he had lost it. Captain Edney heard him with deep concern. He had all along felt a sense of responsibility for the boy Mrs. Manly had intrusted to him, as well as a genuine affection for him; he had therefore double cause to be pained by this unexpected development.

"Frank," said he, "I am glad I did not first hear this story from any body else; and I am glad that the proof of your thorough repentance accompanies the confession. That breaks the pain of it. To-morrow I will see what can be done about the watch. Perhaps we shall get it again. To-night I have only one piece of advice to give. Don't think of winning it back with cards."

"Then how shall I ever get it?" asked Frank, in despair. For he did not wish his mother to know of the circumstances; and to buy the watch back when he was paid off again, would be to withhold money which he felt belonged to her.

Captain Edney could not solve the difficulty; and with that burden upon his mind, Frank returned to his bunk with his letters.

He bent over them with doubt and foreboding. The first he selected was from his mother. As he opened it, his eye caught these words : —

" . . . He says that you beat some of the worst men in the regiment at their own vices. He says you are generally smoking, except when you take out your pipe to swear. According to his account, you are one of the profanest of the profane. And he tells of your going with others to steal turkeys of a secessionist in Maryland, and how you got out of the scrape by the most downright lying. He gives the story so circumstantially that I cannot think he invented it, but am compelled to believe there is something in it. O, my child, is it possible? Ill as your sister is, to hear these things of you is a greater trial than the thought of parting with her so soon. Have you forgotten your promises to me? Have you forgotten —— "

Frank could read no more. He gnashed his teeth together, and held them tight, like a person struggling against some insupportable pain. His sister so ill? That was Hattie. He saw the name written farther back. "He says," — "according to his account," — who was it sending home such stories about him? He glanced up the page, until his eye fell upon the name.

"*John Winch* —— "

O, but this was too much! To be accused of swearing by *him!* To be charged with stealing by one who went with him to steal, and did not, only

because he was a coward! Frank felt an impulse to
fall instantly upon that wretched youth, and choke the
unmanly life out of him. John was at that moment
writing a letter under the lantern, probably filling it
with more tales about him;—and couldn't he tell
some great ones now!—grinning, too, as he wrote;
quite unaware what a tiger was watching him, athirst
for his blood.

Yes, Winch had got letters to-day, and, learning
what a lively sensation his stories of Frank created,
had set to work to furnish the sequel to them; giving
interesting particulars up to latest dates.

N. B. He was writing on the head of Frank's
drum, which he had borrowed for the purpose. He
had written his previous letters on the same. It was
a good joke, he thought, to get the boy he was abus-
ing to contribute some needful assistance towards the
work; it added a flavor to treachery. But Frank did
not so much enjoy the pleasantry. He was wild to be
beating the tattoo, not on the said drum, but on the
head of the rogue who was writing on the drum, and
with his fists for drumsticks.

But he reflected, "I shall only be getting deeper
into trouble, if I pitch into him. Besides, he is a good
deal bigger than I,"—a powerful argument in favor of
forbearance. "I'll wait; but I'll be revenged on him
some way."

Little did he know — and as little did Winch surmise — how that revenge was to be accomplished. But it was to be, and soon.

For the present, Frank had other things to think of. He read of Hattie's fading away; of her love for him; and the tender messages she sent, — perhaps the last she would ever send to him. And he remembered his wonderful vision of her that evening. And tears came to cool and soften his heart.

And so we quit him for the night, leaving him alone with his letters, his grief, and his remorse.

XIX.

SETH GETS "RILED."

THERE is in the life of nearly every young person a turning-point of destiny. It may be some choice which he makes for himself, or which others make for him, whether of occupation, or companion, or rule of life. It may be some deep thought which comes to him in solitary hours, — some seed of wisdom dropped from the lips of teacher, parent, or friend, sinking silently as starlight into the soul, and taking immortal root there, unconsciously, perhaps, even to himself. Now it is the quickening of the spirit at the sight of God's beautiful universe — a rapture of love awakened by a morning in spring, by the blue infinity of the sky, by the eternal loneliness and sublimity of the sea. Or, in some moment of susceptibility, the smiles of dear home faces, the tender trill of a voice, a surge of solemn music, may have power over the young heart to change its entire future. And again, it is some vivid experience of temptation and suffering that shapes the great hereafter. For the Divinity that

(202)

maketh and loveth us is forever showering hints of beauty and blessedness to win back our wandering affections, — dropping cords of gentlest influences to draw home again all hearts that will come.

Then the spirit of the youth rises up within him, and says, —

"Whereas I was blind, now I am beginning to see. And whereas I was weak, now, with God's help, I will strive for better things. Long enough have I been the companion of folly, and all the days of my life have I been a child. But now I perceive that I am to become a man, and I will henceforth think the thoughts and do the deeds of a man."

Such an experience had come to Frank; and thus, on the new morning, as he beheld it rise out of the sea, his spirit spake unto him.

He answered his mother's letter, confessing that his conduct had afforded only too good a foundation for Jack's stories.

"The trouble, I think, is," said he, "that I wrote my promises first with *a pencil.* They did get a little *rubbed out* I own. I have since taken *a pen*, and written them all over again, word by word, and letter by letter, *with ink.* So you may depend upon it, dear mother, that not another syllable of my pledge will *get blurred* or *dimmed*, either on the *leaf of my Testament*, or on the *page of my heart.* Only *believe this*, and then you may believe as much as you please of what *J. W.* writes."

Not a word to the same *J. W.* did Frank say of the base thing he had done; and as for the revenge he had vowed, the impulse to wreak it in tigerish fashion had passed like a night-fog before the breezy purity of the new life that had dawned.

In a couple of days Frank had mostly recovered his equanimity. The loss of the watch was still a source of anxious grief to him, however; less on his own account, let me say, than for the sake of the unknown giver. Nor had he, as yet, found any opportunity to atone for his rudeness to the old drum-major, who had lately, for some cause, gone over to the other wing of the regiment on board the steamer, so that Frank yearned in vain to go to him and humbly beg forgiveness for his fault.

"What has taken Mr. Sinjin away?" he asked of his friend, the young corporal.

Gray shrugged his shoulders, and looked at Frank as if he had a good mind to tell a secret.

"How should I know? He's such a crotchety old boy. I don't think he could account for his conduct himself. He asked permission to remove his quarters to the steamer, and got it; pretending, I believe, that he could have better accommodations there."

"And *I* believe," said Frank, "that you know more about it than you will own."

"Well, I have my suspicions. Shall I be candid with you, Frank? and you'll forgive me if I hurt your feelings?"

"Yes," said Frank, anxiously.

"Well, then," said Gray, "I suppose you know Sinjin had taken a great fancy to you."

"I thought at one time he liked me."

"At one time? I'll wager my head he was liking you the most when he appeared to the least — he's such a queer old cove! I've heard he was disappointed in love once, and that some friend of his proved traitor to him; and that's what has made him so shy of showing any thing like affection for any body. Well, he heard of your gambling, and went to talk with you about it, and you said something to him that wounded him so I think he couldn't bear the sight of you afterwards."

The boy's heart was wrung by this revelation. What reason, he demanded to know, had Gray for thinking thus?

"Because I know the man, and because I know something which I think you ought to know." Gray drew Frank confidentially aside. "He may anathematize me for betraying his secret; but I think it is time to do him justice, even against his will. Frank, it was Old Sinjin who gave you the watch."

Frank's heart leaped up, but fell again instantly, convulsed with pain and regret.

"Are you sure, Gray?"

" Sure as this: I was with him when he bought the watch in Annapolis. I helped him do it up in the wrappers. And it was I that pitched it into the tent at you Thanksgiving-day evening. That is being pretty sure — isn't it?"

"And he knows that I lost it?" said Frank.

" He had just heard so when he went to speak with you about gambling."

" And I told him it was none of his business," said Frank, remorsefully. " O, he will never forgive me now; and who can blame him? Good old man! dear, good old man! My mother told me to be always very kind to him — and how have I repaid his goodness to me!"

It seemed now that the boy could not control his impatience until once more he had seen his benefactor, confessed all to him, and heard him say he was forgiven for his unkindness and ingratitude.

But the old drummer still remained on board the steamer. And Frank had only this faith to comfort him — that if his repentance was sincere, and he henceforth did only what was right, all would yet be well.

The next morning he was viewing the sunrise from the deck, when Seth Tucket came to his side.

" ' Once more upon the waters! yet once more! and the waves bound beneath me as the steed that knows his rider — welcome to their roar! ' Only they don't bound much, and they don't roar to-day," said Seth. " The boys have found out it's Sunday; and as we're to have a battle 'fore the week's out, they seem to think it's about as well to remember there's a difference in days. How are you, Manly? "

" Better," said Frank, with a smile.

" Happy? " — with a grimace meant to be sympathizing, but which was droll enough to be laughable.

" Happier than I was," said the drummer boy. " Happier than I've been for a long time."

" What! not happier, now you've lost every thing, than when you was hevin' such luck at play? "

" I wasn't happy then. I thought I was. But I was only excited. I am happier now that I've lost every thing; it's true, Tucket."

" Well, I swan to man! I thought you was mourning over your luck, and I was bringing ye sunthin' to kind o' cheer ye up. Glad to hear you've no need. Fine day, but rather windy. Wonder what's the time! "

So saying, Seth drew out the watch, and regarded it with provoking coolness.

"I'm plagued ef the darned thing hain't run down! Say, Frank, ye couldn't think of throwin' in the key, too — could ye? I can't wind her up without a key."

Frank choked a little, but his look was cheerful, as he put his hand in his pocket, and, without a word, delivered over to the new owner of the watch the key also.

"Thank ye; much obleeged;" and Seth "wound her up" with extraordinary parade. Then he shook it, and held it to his ear. Then he said, "All right! she's a puttin' in again, lickety-switch! Good watch, that." Then he set it "by guess." Then he was returning it to his pocket, when a new thought seemed to strike him.

"What do ye do for a watch-pocket, Frank? Gov'-ment don't provide watch-pockets, seems."

"I made one for myself," said Frank.

"Sho now! ye didn't, though — did ye? What with?"

"With a needle and thread I brought from home, and with another old pocket," said Frank.

"Well, you air the cutest! Say, what'll ye tax to make me one? I don't care to hev it very large; a small watch, so."

A dry proposal, that. It was not enough to furnish watch and watch-key; but Frank was required also to provide a watch-pocket.

"What do ye say?" asked Seth, with a shrewd squint.

"I'll make you one for nothing," said Frank.

"Come, by darn!" exclaimed Seth; "none o' that, now!"

"None of what?"

"You're a-trying my disposition!"—And, indeed, Tucket was visibly moved; there was a tear in his eye — a bona fide tear. "I've a good disposition, nat'rally; but I shall git riled ef you say much more. I've got your watch, and that's all right. I've got the key, and that's all right, too. But when you talk of makin' a watch-pocket for nothin', I tell ye a saint couldn't stand that."

Frank, who thought he had learned to know pretty well the man's oddities, was puzzled this time.

"I didn't mean to offend you, Tucket."

"No, you didn't. And now see here, Manly. We'll jest compromise this matter, ef you've no 'bjection. I've no watch-pocket, and you've no watch. So, s'posin' you carry the watch for me, and tell me what time it is when I ax ye? That won't be too much trouble — will it?"

"Are you in earnest?" asked Frank.

14

"Yes, I be, clean up to the hub. The truth is, I can't carry that watch with any kind o' comfort, and I'm bent on gitt'n' it off my hands, ef I hef to throw it overboard. Here! It's yours; take it, and be darned!" said Seth.

"I was going to propose to you," — stammered Frank from his too full heart, — "to take the watch, and pay you for it when I can."

"Ez for that, the pay's no consequence. I was more to blame than you; and the loss ought to be mine."

"But —— " insisted Frank.

"No buts! Besides, I never make bargains Sundays." And Seth turned away abruptly, leaving the watch in Frank's hand.

The boy would have called him back, but a rush of emotions — joy, gratitude, contrition — choked his voice. A dash of tears fell upon the watch as he gazed on it, and pressed it, and would have kissed it, had he been alone. It was his again; and that, after all, was an unalloyed satisfaction. He could lie awake nights and study days to devise means to reward Seth's generosity. And he would do it, he resolved. And Mr. Sinjin should know that he had recovered the prize, and that he held it all the more precious since he had found out the giver.

XX.

SUNDAY BEFORE THE BATTLE.

FRANK was leaning over the rail of the schooner, gazing down at the beautiful flashing water, and thinking of home. It was Sunday there, too, he remembered; and he could almost hear the sweet-toned bells solemnly chiming, and see the atmosphere of Sabbath peace brooding over field and village, and feel the serious gladness of the time. The folks were getting ready for church. There was his father, shaved and clean, in his black stock and somewhat threadbare, but still respectable, best coat. And there was Helen, bright and blooming, with her bonnet on, and with her Bible and question-book in her hand, setting out for the morning Sunday-school. His mother was not going to meeting; she was to stay at home with Hattie, and read to her, or, what was better, comfort her with affectionate, gentle, confiding words. But Willie was going with Helen, as he seemed anxious, by strut, and hurry, and loud, impatient talk, to let every body know. And Frank wished from his

heart that he could be with them that day; and he
wondered, did they miss him, and were they thinking
of him, far off here in Carolina waters, alone in the
midst of such crowds of men?

"Wouldn't I like to be in that boat, boys!" said
Ellis. "Don't she come dancing on the waves!"

"She's pulling towards us," said Atwater. "I believe they're coming aboard."

"O, Atwater!" cried Frank, as the boat drew near.
"There's a face there I know! One you know, too!"
And he clapped his hands with joy; for it was a face
he had seen in Boston, and he felt that it came with
news from home.

The rare brightness kindled in Atwater's eyes as he
gazed, and remembered. The boat came alongside,
and hailed the schooner. And a man in the bow, as it
rose upon a wave, seizing hold of the ladder of tarred
rope, stepped quickly upon it, and came on board,
cordially received by Captain Edney, who appeared
to have been expecting him.

"It's the minister that married Atwater!" the rumor
ran round among the troops. "What's his name,
Frank?"

"His name's Egglestone," said Frank, his heart
swelling with anxiety to speak with him.

The minister had come on a mission of Christian
love to the soldiers of the expedition; and having, the

day before, sent word to Captain Edney of his arrival, he had in return received an invitation to visit the schooner and preach to the men this Sunday morning.

A previous announcement that religious services would probably be held on board, had excited little interest; the troops surmising that the chaplain of the regiment, who had never been with them enough to win their hearts or awaken their attention, was to rejoin them, and preach one of his formal discourses.

But far different was the feeling when it was known that the " man that married Atwater" was to conduct the exercises. Then the soldiers remembered that they were New Englanders; and that here also God's Sabbath shed its silent influence, far though they were from the rude hills and rocky shores of home.

'Tis curious how a little leaven of memory will sometimes work in the heart. Here was half a regiment of men, who had come to fight the battles of their country. As with one accord they had left the amenities of peaceful life behind them, and assumed the rugged manners of war. Of late they had seemed almost oblivious of the fact that God, and Christain worship, and Christian rules of life were still in existence. But to-day they were reminded. To-day the child was awakened — the child that had known the wholesome New England nurture, that had sat on mother's knee, and had its earliest thought tuned to

the music of Sunday bells; the child that lay hidden
in the deep heart of every man of them, the same
lived again, and looked forth from the eyes, and smiled
once more in the softened visage of the man. And
the man was carried back, far from these strange
scenes, far from the relentless iron front of war, across
alien lands, and over stormy seas, — carried back by
the child yearning within, — to the old door yard, the
village trees, the family fireside, the family pew, and
the hushed congregation.

It was Mr. Egglestone's aim, in the beginning of
the sermon he preached that morning, to remind the
soldiers of their childhood. "It is a thought," he
said, "which almost moves me to tears, — that all
these hardy frames around me were but the soft,
warm, dimpled forms of so many infants once. And
nearly every one of you was, I suppose, watched over
by tender parents, who beheld, with mutual joy, the
development of each beautiful faculty. The first step
taken by the babe's unassisted feet, the first articulate
word spoken by the little lisping lips, — what delight
they gave, and how long were they remembered! And
what thoughts of the child's future came day and night
to those parents' breasts! and of what earnest prayers
was it the subject! And of all the parents of all those
children who are here as men to-day, not one foresaw
a scene like this; none dreamed that they were raising

up patriots to fight for freedom's second birth on this continent, in the most stupendous of civil wars.

"But Providence leads us by strange ways, and by hidden paths we come upon brinks of destiny which no prophet foresaw. Now the days of peace are over. Many of you who were children are now the fathers of children. But your place is not at home to watch over them as you were watched over, but to strive by some means to work out a harder problem than any ever ciphered on slates at school."

Then he explained to his audience the origin of the war; for he believed it best that every soldier should understand well the cause he was fighting for. He spoke of the compact of States, which could not be rightfully broken. He spoke of the serpent that had been nursed in the bosom of those States. He related how slavery, from being at first a merely tolerated evil, which all good men hoped soon to see abolished, had grown arrogant, aggressive, monstrous; until, angered by resistance to its claims, it had deluged the land with blood. Such was the nature of an institution based upon selfishness and wrong. And such was the bitter result of building a LIE into the foundations of our national structure. Proclaiming to the world, as the first principle of our republican form of government, that "all men are created free and equal," we had at the same time held a race in bondage.

"Neither nation nor individual," said he, " can in any noble sense succeed, with such rotten inconsistency woven into its life. It was this shoddy in the garment of our Goddess of Liberty, which has occasioned the rent which those needles there"—pointing to some bayonets—"must mend. And it is this shoddy of contradiction and infidelity which makes many a man's prosperity, seemingly substantial at first, promising warmth and wear, fall suddenly to pieces, and leave his soul naked to the winds of heaven."

It was not so much a sermon as a friendly, affectionate, earnest talk with the men, whom he sought to counsel and encourage. There was a melting love in his tones which went to their inmost souls. And when he exhorted them to do the work of men who feared God, but not any mortal foe, who dreaded dishonor, but not death, he made every heart ring with the stirring appeal.

Then suddenly his voice sank to a tone of solemn sweetness, as he said,—

"Peace! O, my brothers! struggle and violence are not the all of life. But God's love, the love of man to man, holiness, blessedness,—it is for these realities we are created, and placed here on this beautiful earth, under this blue sky, with human faces and throbbing human hearts around us. And the end of all is PEACE. But only through fiery trial and valiant doing can any peace worth the name come to us; and to make the future truly blessed, we must make the present truly brave."

Before and after the discourse the men sang some of the good old tunes which all had been familiar with at home, and which descended like warm rain upon the ground where the scattered seed of the sermon fell.

The services ended, Mr. Egglestone went freely among the soldiers, and conversed with any who wanted to have speech of him; especially with Atwater; whose wife he had seen a few days before leaving Boston, where she came to see him, having learned who he was, and that he was about departing for the army in which her husband served.

After long waiting, Frank's turn came at last. They sat down on a bench apart; and the clergyman told him he had lately seen his mother, and that she had charged him with many messages. And one was a message of sorrow.

" She had heard unwelcome news of you," he said, holding the boy's hand. " And she wished me to say to you what I could to save you from what she dreads most — what any wise, loving mother dreads most for her child. But is there need of my saying any thing? By what your captain tells me, and still more by what your face tells me, I am convinced that I may spare my words. You have had in your own experience a better lesson than any body can teach you. You have erred, you have suffered. And"—he took a letter from his pocket—"I have something here to make you remember what you have learned—I think, for always."

Frank had listened, humbly, tremblingly, full of tears which he did not shed for the eyes that were about them. But now he started, and took the letter eagerly. "What's it? any bad news?" for he felt an alarming presentiment.

"I do not think it is bad. If you had seen what I saw, you would not think so either." Mr. Egglestone's manner was exceedingly tender, and his voice was liquid and low. "All is well with your folks at home; both with those who are there as you left them, and with the one whose true home is not there any longer, but in a brighter land, we trust."

"O!"—it was almost a cry of pain that broke from Frank. "Hattie?"

"Yes, Frank; it is of Hattie I am speaking. She has passed away. I was present, and saw her depart. And she was very calm and happy, and her last look was a smile, and her last words were words of hope and love. The letter will tell you all about it. I recall one thing, however, which I will repeat, since it so nearly concerns you. They were speaking of you. And she said, 'Maybe I shall see him before any of you will! Yes!' she added, her face shining already like a spirit's with the joyful thought, 'tell him how I love him; and say that I shall be with him when he does not know!' And I am sure that, if it is possible for souls that have escaped from these environments of flesh to be near us still, she will often be near you, loving you, influencing you. Perhaps she is present now, and hears all we say, and sees how badly you feel, and thinks you would not feel quite so badly if you knew that she is happy."

Frank would have spoken, to ask some earnest question which arose in his heart; but his feelings were too much agitated, and he could not trust his voice.

"We will believe such things are true of our lost ones," Mr. Egglestone said, with a parting pressure of the boy's hand. "For, with that faith, we shall surely try so to live that, when they approach us, they will not be repelled; and thus we will be guarded from evil, if not by any direct influence of theirs, then by our own reverence and love for them."

With this he took his leave. And Frank crept into his bunk, and turned away his face, before he dared to open and read his mother's letter.

In that letter there were no reproofs for his misconduct. But in place of such his mother had written the simple story of Hattie's death, with many affecting little details, showing her thoughtful tenderness for all, her cheerful sweetness, and her love for Frank. Then followed affectionate messages from them at home, who were very lonely now, and longed to have him with them — all which had a power beyond any reproaches to win the boy back to that purity of heart and life which belonged to his home-affections, and was safe when they were strong, and was imperilled when they were forgotten.

"O, to think," he said to himself, "only this morning I was imagining how it looked at home to-day — and it is all so different! I am gone, and now Hattie is gone too!"

XXI.

UP THE SOUND.

So passed that Sunday, memorable to the expedition; for it ushered in the battle-week.

Besides the transports and store-ships belonging to the coast division, a squadron of United States gunboats, under command of Commodore Goldsborough, had rendezvoused at the inlet. These were to take care of the rebel fleet, attend to the shore batteries, and prepare the way for the operation of the land forces.

All the vessels destined to take part in the advance were now over the bulkhead, in Pamlico Sound. On Monday, the sailing vessels were hauled into position, each astern of its steam-consort, by which it was to be towed. Sixty-five vessels of various classes were to participate in the movement; while upwards of fifty were to remain behind at the inlet, holding in reserve sixty days' supply of stores for the entire expedition.

The stay at the inlet had occasionally been enlivened by the arrival of refugees, white and black, from

the coast of North Carolina. Some of these were citizens escaped from the persecutions meted out by the
rebels to all who still remained loyal to the old flag.
Some were deserters from the confederate army, in
which they had been compelled to serve. Others
were slaves fleeing from bondage to freedom.

Again, on Monday, a sail-boat hove in sight, and,
being overhauled by one of the gunboats, proved to
be loaded with these fugitives. They were mostly
negroes; two of whom were bright, intelligent boys,
who gave such evidence of joy at their escape, of loy-
alty to the Union, and of a thorough knowledge of
the country, that Flag-officer Goldsborough retained
them for the information they might be able to give,
while the rest were sent ashore.

And now, general orders were read to the troops,
announcing to them that they were soon to land on
the coast of North Carolina, and reminding them that
they were there, not to pillage or destroy private
property, but to subdue the rebellion, and to maintain
the Constitution and the laws.

Monday and Tuesday were occupied with preparations. But early Wednesday morning — more than
three weeks after the arrival of the expedition at the
inlet — the signals to weigh anchor and set sail were
given.

Commodore Goldsborough's gunboat took the lead.

Other vessels of the naval squadron followed. Then came the transports — a goodly spectacle.

"'T were wuth ten years of peaceful life, one glance at our array,'" observed the poetical Tucket.

Each brigade formed three columns of steamers and sailing vessels in tow; and brigade followed brigade. The shallow water of the sound was scarcely ruffled by a breeze. It lay like a field of silver before the furrows of the fleet. The tall, taper masts of the schooners pointed like needles to the sky under which they moved. The aisles between the three columns of ships were unbroken through the whole length of the fleet, which extended for two miles over the surface of the sound, and advanced with such slow and uniform motion, each vessel keeping its position, that now all seemed moving as one, and again all seemed at rest, with the waters of the sound flowing past their steady keels.

As yet, the destination of the fleet was unknown. As it proceeded at first southward and westward, the rumor grew that Newbern was to be attacked. But it was only the course of the channel which thus far shaped its course; and after a few zigzag turns, the cause of which was inexplicable to the green ones, ignorant of the shoals, it began to steer due north. Then all doubts with regard to its destination vanished.

"Roanoke Island, boys! Roanoke Island!" was echoed from mouth to mouth on board the schooner.

The day was beautiful — only a light breeze blowing, and a few light clouds floating in the blue ether. And now the vessels at the inlet began to sink below the horizon; first, the hulls, then the decks disappeared; and lastly, spars and rigging went down behind the curve of the sphere, and were visible no more to the clearest glass.

At the same time emerged in the west the main land of North Carolina. At first, tall cypresses rose to view, growing as it were "out of a mirror." Then appeared the long swampy shores, lying dim and low, with here and there a miserable fish-house, the sole trace of human habitation.

At sundown the fleet was within ten miles of Roanoke Island. The signal from the flag-ship was given, at which the vessels of each brigade drew together, the clank of running-out chains sounded along the lines, the anchors plashed, and the fleet was moored for the night.

As yet there were no signs of rebels. What the morrow, what the night, might bring forth was all uncertainty. The night set in dark enough. But soon the sky cleared, the moon came out resplendent, and the stars looked down from their far eternal calm upon the evanescent shows of mortal conflict — the batteries of the rebellion yonder, and here the fleet, no more than the tiniest shells to those distant, serene, awful eyes of Deity. And Frank looked up at the stars; and the spirit within him said, "They will shine the same to-morrow night, and the next night, and forever; and whether there is war or peace, whether victory comes or defeat, and whether thou, child, art living or art dead, they know not, they change not, neither do they rejoice or mourn." And the thought sank deep into the heart of the boy as he retired to his bed, and closed his eyes to sleep.

A sharp lookout was kept for the rebel gunboats all night, but they never made their appearance. The next morning the weather was heavy — promising rain. At eight o'clock, however, the signal to weigh anchor — the Union Jack at the foremast, and the American flag at the stern — was telegraphed from the flag-ship, and repeated by the flag-ship of each brigade. Again the fleet got in motion, approaching the entrance to Croatan Sound. The water was shoal, and progress was slow, and soon it came on to rain. It was a dismal day; rain on the decks, rain on the water, rain on the marshy shores of the main land, and over the forests beyond, where the ghosts of blasted trees stretched their naked arms despairingly to the dripping clouds. And now a low swampy point of

15

Roanoke Island pushes out into the dim water, under a veil of rain.

At about noon, most of the vessels came to anchor. But some of the gunboats advanced to the entrance of Croatan Sound, and reconnoitred. The rebel fleet was discovered, drawn up in line of battle on the west side of the island, awaiting the conflict. A fog coming on, active operations against the enemy were postponed, and the gunboats, withdrawing also, came to anchor for the night.

During the day, several of the armed steamers, which had served as transports, prepared to coöperate with the naval squadron in their true character as gunboats; the troops on board of them being distributed among other vessels of the coast division. Among the steamers thus cleared was the schooner's consort; and thus it happened that Mr. Sinjin returned to his old quarters, to the great joy of the drummer boy, whose heart burned within him at the thought of meeting his old friend once more, after their unhappy parting.

They met, indeed; but the schooner was now so crowded, and such was the stir on board, that Frank scarce found an opportunity to offer the veteran his hand, and get one look out of those serious gray eyes.

The drummers being assembled, the surgeon came to them, and gave each a strip of red flannel to tie on his arm as a token, at the same time informing them that, when the troops landed, they were to go with him and help carry the wounded.

"This begins to look like serious business, my boy," said the old drummer, kindly, as he stooped to assist Frank in tying on his badge.

His touch was very gentle. Frank's breast began to swell. But before he could speak the old man had disappeared in the crowd.

"He don't know yet that I know he gave me the watch," thought the boy, "and he wouldn't look and see that I have it again."

Then he regarded the red token on his arm, and remembered that they all had other things to think of now.

Picket-boats were out in advance all night, at the entrance to Croatan Sound, in the darkness and fog, keeping watch for the enemy. No enemy appeared. Towards morning, however, the fog lifting, two rebel steamers were seen hastily taking to their heels, having come down in the obscurity to see what they could see.

It was Friday, the 7th of February. The morning was beautiful; the sunrise came in clouds of glory; there was as yet no taint of battle in the purity of the air. It was a lovely day for a sea fight. Frank climbed into the rigging to observe.

At ten o'clock Goldsborough's gunboats could be seen making their way, one by one, cautiously, through the narrow channel between marshy islands into Croatan Sound. There were nineteen of them. The gunboats of the coast division followed, six in number. The S. R. Spaulding, to which Burnside had transferred his flag, next went in, making signals for the transports to follow.

Far off a gun was heard. It was only a signal fired by a rebel steamer to announce the approach of the squadron; but it thrilled the hearts of the troops waiting to go into battle.

An hour later another cannon boomed, nearer and louder. It was a shot tossed from the commodore's flag-ship at the rebels, who promptly responded.

The flag-ship now hoisted the signal, —

"THIS DAY OUR COUNTRY EXPECTS EVERY MAN TO DO HIS DUTY."

From ship to ship, from man to man, from heart to heart, thrilled the electric message. It was greeted by cheers and the thunder of guns. This was at half past eleven o'clock.

XXII.

THE ATTACK OF THE GUNBOATS.

THE spars of the transports were beginning to be thronged. Corporal Gray brought up a glass to Frank.

"O, good!" cried Frank. "Is it yours?"

"No; it belongs to Mr. Sinjin."

"Did he send it to me?"

"Not he! But he had been casting that sharp eye of his up at you, and I knew what he meant when he said, 'Corporal, there's a good lookout from the mast-head, if you'd like to take a glass up there."

"Did he really mean it for me, after all my bad treatment of him?" said Frank. "Bless his old heart!"

With his naked eye for the general view, and the glass to bring out the details, Frank enjoyed a rare spectacle that day. Roanoke Island and its surroundings lay outspread before him like a map. On the west of it was Croatan Sound, separating it from the marshes and forests of the main land. On the east was Roanoke Sound, a much narrower sheet of water; beyond which stretched that long, low, interminable strip of land which forms the outer coast, or seaboard, of this double-coasted country. Still east of that glimmered the blue rim of the Atlantic, a dozen miles away. At about the same distance, on the north, beyond Roanoke Island and the two sounds each side of it, opened the broad basin of Albemarle Sound, like an inland sea. The island itself appeared to be some twelve miles in its greatest length, and two or three in breadth, indented with numerous creeks and coves, and forming a slight curve about Croatan Sound. It was within this curve that the naval battle took place. It had now fairly begun.

At noon the flag-officer's ship displayed the signal for closer action, and the engagement soon became general.

The enemy's gunboats, seven in number, showed a disposition to fight at long range, retreating up the sound as the fleet advanced — a movement which soon brought the latter under the fire of a battery that opened from the shore.

The air, which had previously been perfectly clear that morning, was now loaded with clouds of smoke, which puffed from a hundred guns, and surging up from the vessels of the squadron, from the rebel gunboats, and from the shore battery, rolled away in broken, sun-illumined masses, wafted by a light northeasterly breeze.

The soldiers in the rigging of the transports could see the flashes burst from the cannons' mouths, the spouted smoke, the shots throwing up high in air the water or sand as they struck, or coming skip-skip across the sound, the shells exploding, and the terrible roar of the battle filled the air.

For a time the fire of the attack was about equally divided between the rebel steamers and the fortification on the island. It was soon discovered, however, that boats had been sunk and a line of piles driven across the channel abreast of the battery, to prevent the farther advance of our gunboats in that direction. Behind those the retreating steamers discreetly withdrew, where they were presently reënforced by several other armed vessels. The gunboats made no attempt to follow, but took positions to give their principal attention to the battery.

The fire from the shore gradually slackened, and thousands of hearts swelled anew as the hour seemed at hand when the troops were to land and carry the works at the point of the bayonet.

Burnside paced the deck of the Spaulding, keeping an eye on the fort, watching the enemy's shots, and looking impatiently for the arrival of the transports. At length they came crowding through the inlet, dropping their anchors in the sound just out of range of the fort. Seen from the gunboats, they were a sight not less astonishing than that which they themselves were coming to witness. Troops, eagerly watching the conflict, crowded the decks and hung upon the rigging like swarms of bees. Ropes, masts, and yards were festooned with the heavy, clinging clusters, which seemed ready to part and fall with their own weight. The effect of the picture was enhanced by the mellow brilliancy of the afternoon sky, against which the dark masses were clearly defined, and by the perfect tranquillity of the water, like a sea of glass mirroring the ships and their loaded spars.

The gunboats sent to the ships the roar of their artillery, and the ships sent back the chorus of thousands of cheering voices for every well-aimed shot.

Frank was in the rigging of the schooner, watching the fight, making drawings to send to his mother, and talking with his comrades, among whom Sinjin's glass passed from hand to hand.

"I tell ye, boys!" remarks Seth Tucket, "this is a leetle ahead of any game of bluff ever I took a hand in! The battery is about used up. S'pose you look at your — my — our watch, Frank, and see how often the darned rebels fire."

"Once in about ten minutes now," Frank informs

him. "O! did you see that shell burst? Right over one of our gunboats!"

"She's aground," says Gray, with the glass. "She can neither use her guns nor get off! A little tug is going to help her."

"Bully for the tug!" says Jack Winch.

"Hurrah! hurrah!" ring the deafening plaudits from the ships.

"What is it?" is eagerly asked.

"The battery's flag-staff is shot away!" shouts Frank at the top of his voice. "Hooray!"

"Some think the flag has been hauled down, to surrender the fort, but it's a mistake," declares Gray. "See! up it goes again on a piece of the pole! And the guns are at it again."

"Where's Burnside?" asks some one. And Tucket quotes, —

"'O, where was Roderick then? One blast upon his bugle horn were worth a thousand men!'"

"He is sending off a boat to the shore yonder, to look for a landing-place. We'll be going in there soon, boys!"

The boat approaches a cove called Ashby's Harbor, taking soundings as it nears the land. On board of her is one of the negro lads, who fearlessly pilots her towards scenes familiar to his days of bondage.

"They'd better keep their eyes skinned!" says

Tucket. "There's rebels in the mash there, I bet ye a dollar!"

The officers of the boat land safely, and reconnoitre. As they are reëmbarking, however, up spring from the tall grass a company of rebels, and flash, flash, goes a volley of musketry.

"I wish somebody had took me up on my bet," says Tucket; "'twould have been a dollar in my pocket."

"They're off; nobody left behind; nobody hurt, I hope," says Gray, watching the boat.

"Look, boys! the rebel works are afire!" is now the cry.

Flames break through the smoke, and the firing slackens on both sides for a short time.

"It's only the barracks, probably, fired by a shell," says Gray. "They've no idea of surrendering. They hold out well!"

The battery is completely enveloped in black smoke, out of which leaps the white puff of the cannon, showing that the gunners are still at work.

"See! the gunboat that was aground is getting off! that's a brave tug that's handling her!" cries Frank. "O!" — an exclamation of surprise and wonder. For just then the gunboat, swinging around so that she can bring her guns to bear, lets fly her broadside, dropping shot and shell right into the smoking battery.

"It's about time," says Jack Winch, "for us boys to go ashore and clean the rebels out. I'm a gitting tired of this slow work."

"You'll get ashore soon enough, and have enough to do when you get there," says Atwater. "There are strong batteries towards the centre of the island, that'll have to be taken when we go in."

"Abe's afraid," mutters Jack to some comrades near him. "Did ye see him, and Frank, and Seth Tucket, reading their Testaments?"

"It was the 'Lady of the Lake' Seth was reading," says Harris. "He carries it in his pocket, and pitches into it odd spells."

"Winch don't know the Lady of the Lake from the Bible!" chimes in Tucket's high nasal voice.

"Yes, I do, too! The Lady of the Lake, that's one of Byron's poems! S'pose I don't know?"

"O, perfectly!" sneers Ellis, amid the laughter Jack's blunder elicits. "And no doubt you'll soon find out who the cowards are among us, if you don't know already."

"What's that, afire, away up the sound, close into the main land?" asks the phlegmatic Atwater.

"I swan, ef 'tan't one of the rebel steamers! She's got disabled, and they've run her ashore. She's all a sheet of fire now!"

"What's that saucy little tug around here for?"

"Burnside's aboard of her. He's coming to see if we're all right. We shall land soon," says Gray.

"See!" cries Frank; "our gunboats are shelling the shore, to make a landing-place for us. I wouldn't like to be in the woods there!"

"I guess Frank wouldn't!" observes Jack. "But I would; I'd like no better fun than to rush right in and skedaddle the rebels with the bayonet; that's the way to do it!"

"The woods are afire! Our shells have set them afire!" cries Ellis. "Look! there come the rebel steamers again, down the western shore. They think they can get down at us, now our gunboats are busy off there."

"When the cat's away the mice will play," says Tucket. "But the kittens are after 'em!"

"There goes Burnside's tug to see what the row is!"

"The battery scarcely fires at all now," says Frank, looking at his watch. "It's twenty minutes since it has fired a shot."

"There goes one! And see! the gunboats are fighting each other now like mad — again!" cries Gray. "They're all so wrapped in smoke you can hardly see one of 'em." — Bang, bang, bang! — "Isn't it grand?"

"A shell burst right over Burnside's tug!" exclaims Frank. "It burst, and sprinkled the water all around it!"

XXIII.

THE TROOPS DISEMBARK. — THE ISLAND.

AT four o'clock the last of the transports had entered the inlet, and rejoined the fleet. Soon after commenced preparations for the landing of the troops. The boats were lowered and manned, and the soldiers, descending from decks and spars, began to crowd into them. Knapsacks were left behind; the men taking with them only their arms, overcoats, canteens, haversacks, and cartridge-boxes, with three days' rations of pork, beef, and hard bread, and forty rounds of ball cartridges. Down both sides of the vessels they passed, in rapid, regular files, pouring into the boats. Their guns were taken as they stepped upon the stairs, and passed down to them as soon as they were embarked. Some took places at the oars; the rest filed in fore and aft. It must have been an amazing spectacle to the enemy to witness these stirring and formidable preparations for finishing the work the gunboats had begun. The troops were jubilant, and eager for battle.

As fast as the boats were filled, they pushed from the stairs to make room for others, and lay upon their oars watching for the signals. These were telegraphed from the flag-ship of each brigade. At the instant, the boats swarmed the water in miniature fleets, with oars flashing, flags flying, and arms gleaming in the sun. Rowing to the flag-ship, or steamer detailed for the purpose, they attached themselves under her stern in two lines as they arrived, each boat taking the painter of the one behind it. Then, at a signal whistle, the steamers started for the shore, each towing its double string of boats.

In the mean time the fight between the fleet and the battery was continued, — rather languidly, however, on the part of the battery; and a couple of light draught gunboats, running in close to the shore, continued shelling the woods about Ashby's Harbor, to cover the landing of the troops.

When the steamers towing in the boats had arrived as near as the depth of water would permit, the signal whistles were sounded, the painters were cast off, the lines of boats broke simultaneously, the rowers took to their oars and pulled with all speed for the shore. As soon as the prows struck, the men jumped out, dashing through mud and water to the land. Many did not wait for the boats to get in, but, in their eagerness to follow their comrades, leaped overboard where the water was up to their waists. Some got stuck in the mire, and were helped out by those who came after them. Six thousand men were thus thrown upon the island at the first disembarkation; while the remainder of the troops on the transports watched the brilliant scene, and cheered lustily when they saw the flag of the Union waving on the shore.

Frank's regiment was not yet disembarked. The boys were still in the rigging, following with eager eyes the movements of the boats. An exciting incident added interest to the scene. Before the boats landed, a body of rebels in ambush, waiting to receive them, were betrayed by the gleam of their muskets. A shell dropped discreetly into their hiding-place, by one of the gunboats, sent them scampering, and the troops landed without opposition.

"It's our turn now, boys!" cried Tucket. And they slipped from the rigging, impatient to leap into the boats, and be put ashore. "I tell ye, won't it feel good to straighten out a fellow's legs once, on dry land!"

The men were generally of Seth's opinion; their long confinement on shipboard having become exceedingly monotonous and tiresome.

Frank was with his company. They loaded the boats to the gunwales. The water was still smooth, save where it was broken into waves and whirling

eddies by the sweep of oars. The men shouted joy-
ously, and waved their caps. Frank stood in the bow,
and swung his cap with the rest. But looking back
across the shining wakes at the forsaken schooner, a
feeling of sadness came over him — a feeling of regret-
ful memory, as of one leaving home.

There she lay, motionless; hull and spars painted
dark against the sunset sky; her rigging, to the finest
cordage, traced in exquisitely distinct lines upon that
shining background — a picture of exceeding loveli-
ness and peace.

As the boats swept down towards the shore, and
the schooner seemed to recede into the flaming west,
the network of cordage became black cobwebs on the
sky, then melted away and vanished altogether. At
the same time, the water, which the boats had trou-
bled, grew smooth again, reflecting the sunset glow,
with the sombre hull and ebon spars painted upon it,
until Frank saw the spectre of a double ship sus-
pended in a double heaven.

And as the last view of the schooner was all
beautiful, so his last thoughts of her were all tender.
He remembered no more against her the hardships of
the voyage, the seasickness, the two gills of water a
day. But that she had borne them faithfully through
storms, that whether they slept or waked she had
not failed them, — this he remembered. And his sis-

ter's death, and all his sufferings and errors, and the peace of soul which had come to him at last, were associated now and henceforth with his memory of the ship swimming there in the illumined horizon. Only for a brief interval, like a wind that comes we know not whence, and goes again we know not whither, touching us with invisible perfumed wings, these thoughts swept over the boy, and passed as quickly. And he turned from gazing after the schooner to face the scenes before him. Nearer and nearer drew the boats to the island. Its woods and shores lay cool and tranquil in the evening light, and the troops there, half-hidden by the tall grass and the trees, were tinted with a gleam of romance.

It was now fast growing dark. Clouds were gathering in the sky. From their edges the last hues of the sunset faded, the moon was hid, and a portentous gloom fell upon the waves. The cannon were still thundering at intervals. The shells flew screaming through the air, and fell bursting on the fort or in the woods. It was now so dark that the flash of the guns had become lurid and sharp, and the meteoric course of the projectiles could be traced by their fiery wake.

Amid this scene the boats entered the cove, and as the prows struck, or before, the excited soldiers leaped out, regardless of mud and water.

"Shouldn't wonder if somebody got a wet foot,"

16

said Tucket, in the midst of the plunging and plash-
ing — himself in up to his hips. " ' A horse ! a horse !
my kingdom for a horse ! ' Here, Manly, take a grip
of my coat tail. I'm longer legged than you."

" I'm all right," said Frank. " I've no gun to carry,
and I can get along." And he floundered on as fast
as the deep, clinging ooze would permit.

" This is what they call the sacred soil ! " observed
Harris. " Just the thing, I should say, to breed rattle-
snakes and rebels."

" I swan to man ! " chimed in Tucket's voice from a
distance, — for his long legs had given him an advantage in the general race, — " there ain't no shore after
ye get to 't. It's nothin' but salt ma'sh, all trod to
pudd'n' by the fellers that have been in ahead of us.
I thought we was to be *landed;* 'stead of that, we're
swamped ! "

The men pushed on, through marsh and swamp,
sometimes in mire and water knee-deep, and now in
tall, rank grass up to their eyes ; the darkness adding
to their dismal prospect.

" By Grimes ! " mutters Jack Winch, " I don't think
an island of this kind is worth taking. It's jest fit for
secesh and niggers, and nobody else."

" We must have the island, because it's a key to the
coast," says Frank.

"I wouldn't talk war, if I couldn't carry a gun," retorts Jack, made-cross by the cold and wet.

"Perhaps before we get through you'll be glad to lend me yours," is Frank's pleasant response, as he hastens forward through grass which waves about his ears or lies trodden and tangled under foot.

"The gunboats have stopped firing," observes Atwater.

In fact, both gunboats and battery were now silent, the former having drawn off for the night.

XXIV.

THE BIVOUAC.

"There's a good time coming, and near, boys! there's a good time coming, and near!" sings out Tucket, holding his head high as he strides along, for he has caught a sight of fires beyond, and the company are now emerging upon a tract of sandy barrens, thinly covered with pines.

A road runs through the island. The advance of the column has already taken possession of it. Skirmishers have been thrown forward into the woods, and pickets are posted on the flanks.

The troops prepare to bivouac for the night. Fires are kindled, and soon the generous flames blaze up, illumining picturesque groups of men, and casting a wild glare far into the depths of the great, black, silent woods. The trees seem to stand out like startled giants, gazing at the unusual scene; and all above and around the frightened shadows lurk, in ghostly boughs, behind dark trunks, among the deep grasses, and in hollows of the black morass.

And the darkness of the night overhangs the army like a vast tent, sombrely flickering.

A dry fence of cypress and pine rails is, without hesitation, appropriated to feed the fires of the bivouac; and the chilled, soaked soldiers gather around them to get warm and dry.

"My brave fellows," says Captain Edney, passing among them, "do the best you can for yourselves for the night. Try to keep warm, and get what rest and sleep you can. You will need all your strength to-morrow."

"To-morrow," observes Winch, with a swaggering, braggart air, "we're going to give the rebels the almightiest thrashing they've had yet! To wade in their blood as deep as I've waded to-night in this mud and water, that's what'll just suit me!"

"The less blood the better, boys," says Captain Edney. "But we must be prepared to shed our own to the last drop, if need be, for we're bound to sweep this island of every traitor to his country, before we leave it. Make up your minds to that, boys!"

There is that in his tone which promises something besides child's play on the morrow. He is calm, serious, spirited, resolute; and the hearts of his men are fired by his words.

The troops are full of jest and merriment as they kick off their shoes, and empty the water out of them,

squeeze their dripping trousers, and, lying on the
ground, toast their steaming legs by the fires.

"I say, le's have a gallus old time to-night, to pay
for our ducking," suggests Jack Winch. "I don't
want to sleep."

"You ought to be off in the swamps, on picket
duty, then," says Harris. "Let them sleep that have
a chance. For my part, I'm going to take the captain's advice. There's no knowing what sounds will
wake us up, or how early."

"The sounds of muskets, I hope; and the earlier the
better," says the valiant Jack. "Dang that shoe! I
believe I've roasted it! Bah! look at Abe there,
diving into his Testament, sure 's you live."

And Winch, perceiving that Atwater paid no attention to the sneer, flung his shoe at him. The
soldier was reading by the light of the flames, when
the missile came, striking the book from his hands.

"Shame, shame!" cried Frank, indignantly. "Jack
Winch, that is too mean."

"O, you go to" —— France, — only Jack used a
worse word, — "with that red rag on your arm! I
don't have any thing to say to non-combatants."

Frank might not have been able to stifle his indignation but for the grave example of Atwater, who
gave no more heed to Jack's shoe than he had given
to his base taunt, but, silently gathering up his book

again, brushed the sand from it, found his place, and resumed his reading, as composedly as if nothing had happened. Neither did Frank say any thing. But Ellis, near whom the shoe had fallen, tossed it back with a threat to consign it to the fire if it came that way again.

"Wonder if my pocket-book got wet any," said Harris, taking out his money and examining it.

"O, you feel mighty proud of your winnings!" said Jack, who seemed bent on picking a quarrel with some one.

"Yes, I do," said Harris. "I'm just so proud of it as this," — reaching something towards the drummer boy. "Here, Frank, is all the money, I believe, that I've won of you. We're going into a fight to-morrow, and nobody knows how we shall come out of it. I want to stand right with every body, if I can."

Frank was too much astonished to accept the money. He seemed to think there was some joke in it.

"I'm in earnest," insisted Harris. "The truth is, I've been ashamed of winning your money, ever since. You didn't mean it, but you've acted in a way to *make* me ashamed."

"I have! How?" Frank was more amazed than ever.

"Because you gave over play, though you had a

chance to try again, and acted as if you had got above such foolish things. It's time we all got above them. You're a good-hearted fellow, Frank, — you've shown that, — and nobody shall say I've robbed you."

Frank took the money with a heart too full for thanks. He thought Harris a fellow of unexampled generosity, never considering how much his own example had had to do with bringing about this most gratifying result.

Atwater stopped reading, and looked over his book at Harris with a smile of pleasure and approval clear as daybreak. But the silent man did not speak.

"Well! the idea of a battle makes some folks awful pious all at once!" was Winch's comment.

Nobody heeded him. As for Frank, with triumph in his heart and money in his fist, he ran barefoot to where Seth Tucket lay sprawled before the blazing rails, feeling of his stockings, to see if they were dry enough to put on.

"Hello, young chap! how goes it?" 'Stranger, what dost thou require? Rest, and a guide, and food and fire.' Get down here and have a toasting. It comes cheap."

Frank sat down, and began counting the money.

"What's all that?" demanded Seth.

"All I owe you, and a little to spare!" cried Frank, elated.

"Sho, ye don't say! See here, Frank! I never meant you should trouble yourself about that. I'm all right, money or no money. I'm an independent sort of nabob — don't need the vile stuff. 'Kings may be great, but Seth is glorious, o'er all the ills of life victorious!' So put it away, and keep it, Frank."

But when the drummer boy told him how he had come by the money, and that it was his wish to settle his accounts before the battle, Tucket screwed up his face with a resigned expression, and received back the loan.

A great weight was now lifted from Frank's mind. The vexing problem, how he was to retain the watch and yet satisfy Seth's rightful claims, was thus happily solved. He could have danced for joy, barefooted, in the grassy sand. And he yearned more than ever now to see Mr. Sinjin, and make up with him.

A few rods off, in the rear of the soldiers' bivouacs, the old drummer could be seen, sitting with a group of officers around a fire of their own. His stockings were hung upon the end of a rail, and he was busy, roasting a piece of pork on the end of a stick, held out at arm's length to the fire. Frank saw that it was no time to speak with him then; so he returned to his place, and sat down to put on his shoes and join those who had not yet been to supper, over their rations.

XXV.

ATWATER.

As the evening wore on, Atwater was observed sitting apart from the rest, unusually silent and grave even for him; gazing at the fire, with the book he had been reading closed and folded thoughtfully between his hands.

Now Frank, following his example, had lately formed the resolution to read a little in the Testament every night, — "if only for his mother's sake." But to-night his Testament was in his knapsack, and his knapsack was on board the schooner.

"I'll borrow Atwater's," he thought; and with this purpose he approached the tall private.

"Sit down here, Frank," said Atwater, with a serious smile. "I want to talk with you."

It was so extraordinary for the phlegmatic Abe to express a wish to talk with any body, that Frank almost felt awed by the summons. Something within him said that a communication of no trivial import was coming. So he sat down. And the tongue of the taciturn was that night, for once in his life, strangely loosened.

"I can't say it to the rest, Frank; I don't know why. But I feel as if I could say it to you."

"Do," said Frank, thrilling with sympathy to the soldier's mysterious emotion. "What is it, Abe?"

For a minute Atwater sat gazing, gazing — not at the fire. Then he lifted from the book, which he held so tenderly, his right hand, and laid it upon Frank's. And he turned to the boy with a smile.

"I've liked you from the first, Frank. Did you know it?"

"If you have, I don't know why," said Frank, deeply touched.

"Nor do I," said the private. "Some we like, and some we don't, without the reason for it appearing altogether clear. I liked you even when you didn't please me very well."

"You mean when —— " began Frank, stammeringly.

"Yes, you know when. It used to hurt me to see and hear you — but that is past."

"I hope so," said Frank, from his heart.

"Yes. And I like you better than ever now. And do you know, Frank, I don't think I could say to you what I am going to, if you hadn't been in trouble yourself, lately? That makes me feel I can come near you."

"O! are you in trouble, Abe?"

"Yes," — with another mild, serious smile. "Not just such trouble as you were in, though. It is nothing on my own account. It is on *hers*." And the soldier's voice sunk, as it always did, when he alluded to his wife.

"You have heard from her?" asked Frank, with sympathizing interest.

"Nothing but good news; nothing but good news," said Atwater, pressing the pocket where his letters were. "I wish you could know that girl's heart. I am just beginning to know it. She has blessed me! She is a simple creature — not so smart as some; but she has, what is better than all that, a heart, Frank!"

Frank, not knowing what else to say, answered earnestly, that he was sure of it.

"She has brought me to know this book," the soldier continued, his features tremblingly alive with emotion. "I never looked into it much before. I never thought much about it — whether it was true or not. But whether it is true or not, there is something in it that reaches me here," — laying his hand on his heart, — "something that sinks into me. I can't tell how. It gives me comfort."

Frank, still not knowing how to reply, murmured that he was glad to hear it.

"Now, this is what I have been wanting to say to somebody," Abram went on, in a calm but suppressed voice. "I am going into battle to-morrow. Don't think I am afraid. I have no fear. But of one thing I am tolerably certain. I shall not come out of that fight unhurt."

The smile which accompanied these words, quite as much as the words themselves, alarmed Frank.

"Don't say that!" he entreated. "You are a little low-spirited, Abe; that's it."

"O, no! I am not low-spirited in the least. My country demands sacrifices. I, for one, am willing to die." This was said with singular calmness and cheerfulness. But the soldier's voice failed him, as he added, "It is only when I think of her ——"

Frank, powerfully wrought upon, endeavored in vain to dissuade his friend from indulging in such sad presentiments.

"Well, we will hope that they are false," said Atwater, but with a look that betrayed how thoroughly he was convinced of their truth. "If I go through safely, then we can laugh at them afterwards. But much may happen in these coming twenty-four hours. Now, I am sitting here with you, talking by these fires that light up the woods so. To-morrow night, this which you call me," — the soldier smilingly designated his body, — "may be stretched upon this

same earth, and you may talk in vain — it cannot
answer you."

"We don't know, — that's true," Frank agreed.
"But I hope for the best."

"And that may be the best — for me. God knows.
And for her, too, — though I dread the stroke for her!
This is what I want you to do for me, Frank. If I
fall, — *if* I fall, you know, — you will write to her.
Send back to her my last words, with the book she
gave me, and her letters. You will find them all in
this pocket, here. Will you?"

Frank could not refrain from tears, as he made the
promise.

"That is all," said Atwater, cheerfully. "Now, my
mind is easier. Now, whatever comes, I am ready.
Stay with me, if you like, and we will talk of something else. Or shall we read a little together?"

"I'd like to read a little," said Frank.

And he opened the book to these words : —

"'Fear not them which kill the body, but are not
able to kill the soul. . . . Are not two sparrows sold
for a farthing? and one of them shall not fall to the
ground without your Father. But the very hairs of
your head are all numbered. Fear not, therefore; ye
are of more value than many sparrows.'"

"How came you to read there?" said Atwater,
with a smile.

"I don't know," said Frank. "But it seems meant for you — don't it?"

"Yes, and it somehow makes me happy. Go on."

And Frank read, —

"'Think not I am come to send peace on earth: I came not to send peace, but a sword.'"

"That is for both of us, for all of us, for all our people to-day," said Atwater. "I believe it is the struggle of Satan against Christ that has brought on this war. To attempt to build up a nation on human slavery — that is Satan. And I believe, wicked as we are at the north too, that the principle of freedom we are fighting for is the opposite of Satan. And whoever brings that into the world, brings a war that will never cease until the right triumphs, and the wrong ceases forever."

Frank was astonished. He had never suspected that in this stiff, reserved soldier there dwelt the spirit which, when their tongues are loosed, makes men eloquent.

Atwater had roused up, and spoken with earnestness. But his glow passed, and he said quietly, —

"Go on."

"'A man's foes shall be they of his own household.'"

There Frank stopped again, this time of his **own** accord. The words struck him with peculiar **force.**

" That is true too," said Abram; " of the nation, for a nation is a household; and of many, many families."

Frank studied the words a moment, and, after a struggle with his feelings, said in a hushed voice, —

" Did you know, Abe, I've a brother in the rebel army ? "

" I did not know. I have heard you have one somewhere in the south."

" Yes, you have heard Jack twit me about my secesh brother. And I have been obliged to own he was a — traitor. And since I left home my folks have had a letter from him, in which he wrote that he was on the point of joining the confederate army, and that we would not probably hear from him again. So I suppose he is fighting against us somewhere."

" Not here, I hope," said Atwater.

" As well here as any where," said Frank. " I always loved my brother. I love him still. But, as you say, wicked as we are, Christ is in our cause, and —— " Frank read, —

" ' He that loveth father or mother more than me, is not worthy of me ; and he that loveth son or daughter more than me, is not worthy of me.' "

" And I," said the boy, lifting up his face with a patriotic, even a religious, fervor in it, " 1 love my country, I love the cause of right and freedom, better than I love my brother ! "

"With that true of us, with that love in our hearts," said Atwater, "we can dare to fight, and whatever the result, I believe it will be well with us. See what the book says."

And Frank read on.

"'He that findeth his life shall lose it; and he that loseth his life for my sake shall find it.'"

"That is enough," said Atwater. "I can bind that sentence like an armor around my heart."

"What does it mean?"

"It means, I think, that though wickedness triumphs, it triumphs to its own confusion, for it has no immortal life. But even the death of a saint is victory."

After that the soldier seemed inclined to relapse into revery. Frank thought he did not wish to talk any more; so he gave him back the book. Abram put it in his pocket, and took the boy's hand.

"Good night, Frank," he smilingly said. "We shall see each other in the morning."

"Good night, Abe."

Frank left him. And Atwater, stretching himself upon the ground, put his arm beneath his head, and with the fire-light on his placid countenance, dismissed all worldly care from his mind, and slept peacefully.

17

XXVI.

OLD SINJIN.

At the foot of a pine tree, on a pillow of boughs, lies the old drum-major. The blaze of the bivouac fire covers him with its glow as with a mantle. But his face looks haggard and care-worn, and his grizzled mustache has a cynical curl even in sleep.

At a sound he starts, opening wide those watchful gray eyes an instant, then closing them quickly. It is a footstep approaching.

Stealthily it comes, and passes by his side. Then silence — broken only by the crackle and roar of the flames. At length one eye of the sleeper opens a little, and peeps; and as it peeps, it sees, sitting on the pine roots, in the broad fire-light, with his cap before his eyes shading them, and his eyes fixed wistfully on him, Frank, the drummer boy.

The eye that opened a little and peeped, closes again. The old fellow begins to snore.

"Poor old man!" says, the boy to himself; "how tired he looks! And to think I have done so much to

hurt his feelings! I wish I could tell him how sorry I am; but I must not wake him."

Again the ambushed eye opens, and the little corner of the sleeper's soul that happens to be *not* asleep, reconnoitres. Frank is sitting there still, faithfully watching. A stream of electric fire tingles in that misanthropic breast, at the sight. But still the old man snores.

"I may as well lie down and go to sleep too," says Frank. And, very softly, so as not to awaken Mr. Sinjin, he lays himself down by his side, puts his cheek on the pillow of boughs, and keeps perfectly still.

The heart of the veteran burns within him, but he makes no sign. And now — hark! Patter, patter, patter. It is beginning to rain.

This, then, is what the dark canopy meant, hanging so luridly over the fire-lit forest. Patter, patter; faster, faster; dripping through the trees, hissing in the fire, capering like fairies on the ground, comes the midnight rain.

Sinjin thinks it about time to wake. But Frank is stirring; so he concludes to sleep a little longer, and see what he will do.

Frank takes some pine boughs, and lays them carefully over the old man, to shelter him from the rain. Hotter and hotter glows the old heart beneath; melt it must soon.

"There!" says Frank in a whisper; "don't tell him I did it!"

He is going. Old Sinjin can sleep — or pretend to sleep — no more.

"Hello! Who's there?" — awaking with amazing suddenness. — "That you, Frank? What are you here for at this time of night?"

"O, I'm a privileged character. They let me go around the camp about as I like, you know."

"How long has it been raining? And how came all this rubbish heaped over me?"

The pattering becomes a rushing in the tree-tops, a wild sibilation as of serpents in the fire, and a steady rattling and whizzing in the swamps.

"Well, well! this won't do, boy! Come with me!"

They run to the shelter of a huge leaning trunk, and crouch beneath it.

"You're not so used to these things as I am," says the old man, shielding the boy with his arms.

"Let me bring some boughs to throw over you!" cries Frank.

"No — sit still! You have heaped boughs enough on me for one night!"

"Were you — awake?"

"One eye was a little awake."

"And you saw!"

"I saw all you did, my boy!"

Frank knows not whether to be happy or ashamed. Neither speaks. The storm is roaring in the trees. The water drips and the spray sifts upon them. At length Frank says, —

"I wanted to tell you I have the watch again, and I know who gave it to me, and I think he is one of the best old men in the world. And I wanted to say that I am very sorry for every thing I have said and done that was wrong."

The bosom of the lonely old man heaves as he answers, "Don't, my boy! don't say you are sorry — I can't stand that!" And he hugs the boy close.

"But why didn't you want me to know you gave the watch?"

"Because I am such a foolish old fellow, and have forgotten how to treat a friend. For twenty years and more I have not known what it was to have a living soul care for me."

"O, it must be so hard for you to be alone so! Have you no sisters?"

"Sisters! I could tell you of one so proud, and rich, and in fashion, that her great house has no room in it for a rusty old brother like me!"

Frank thought of his own sisters — of Hattie, who was gone, and of Helen, who, though she should wed a prince, would never, he was sure, shut her doors against him; and he was filled with pity for the poor old man.

"But you must have had friends?"

"I had one, who was a fast friend enough when he was poor and I had a little property. But I became responsible for his debts, which he left me to pay; then I was poor, whilst he grew rich and hated me!"

"Hated you?"

"Of course! We may forgive those who wrong us, but not those we have wronged. He never forgave me for having been robbed by him!" And the old man's voice grew hard and ironical at the recollection.

"Why didn't you ever get married?" asked Frank. "You have one of the best, biggest hearts in the world, and you ought to have loved somebody with it. Didn't you ever?"

The spirit of the old man shrank sensitively within him for a moment. Then he said to himself, "He will know of it some day, and I may as well tell him." For the heart that had been frozen for years this youth had had power to thaw.

"I never loved — any woman — well enough to marry her. But there was once a little girl that I had known from her cradle — for I was many years older than she. I used to pet her, and tell her stories, and sing and play to her, until I became more bound up in her than was very wise for one who was not her father or her brother. Well, she got to be of your age, and still ran to kiss me when I came, and never guessed what was growing up in my heart and taking possession of me, for it was stronger than I, and stronger than all the world. I saw her fast becoming a woman, and forgot that I was at the same time fast becoming an old man. And one day I asked her to marry me. I did not mean then, but in a few years. But she did not stop to hear my explanations. She sprang from me with a scream. And that ended it. She could never be to me again the innocent pet she had been, and as for being what I wished — I saw at once how absurd the proposal was! I saw that from that time she could regard me only with astonishment and laughter. I was always extremely sensitive, and this affair, with the other I have told you of, proved too much for me. I fled from society. I enlisted as a drummer, and I suppose I shall never be any thing but a drummer now. And this, my boy, is the reason I was never married."

Drearily sounded the old man's voice as he closed.

"It is all so sad!" said Frank. "But ought a man to do so, because he has been once or twice deceived? I have heard my mother say that as we are to others, so they will be to us. If we are generous, that excites them to be generous; and love calls out love."

"Your mother says that?" replied Mr. Sinjin in a low voice. "Ah, and she says true! If one is proud and reserved, he will find the world proud and reserved: that I know! Because two or three failed me, I distrusted every body, and was repaid with distrust. O my boy, do not do so! Never let your soul be chilled by any disappointment, if you would not become a solitary and neglected old man. Better trust a thousand times, and be deceived as often, better love a thousand times in vain, than shut up your heart in suspicion and scorn. Your mother is right, Frank,—in that, as in every thing else, she is perfectly right!"

"It isn't too late yet—is it?—to have friends such as you like. I am sure you can if you will," said Frank.

"You have almost made me think so," answered the old drummer. "You have brought back to my heart more of its youth and freshness than I had felt for years. I want you to know that, my boy."

Frank did not understand how it could be, and the old man did not inform him. It was now very late. The rain poured dismally. Frank lay nestled in the old man's bosom, like a child. For a long time he did not speak. Then the veteran bent forward so that he could look in his face. The boy was fast asleep.

"How much he looks like his mother! Her brow, her mouth! God bless the lad, God bless him!"

And the old man sat and watched whilst the drummer boy slept.

XXVII.

THE SKIRMISH.

·

THE night and the storm passed, and day dawned on Roanoke Island.

No reveillé roused up the soldiers. Silently from their drenched, cold beds, they arose and prepared for the rough day's work before them.

The morning was chill and wet, the rain still dripping from the trees. Far in the cypress swamps the lone birds piped their matin songs — the only sounds in those dim solitudes, so soon to be filled with the roar of battle.

Ten thousand men had been landed from the fleet; and now ten thousand hearts were beating high in anticipation of the conflict.

The line of advance lay along the road, which ran in a northerly direction through the centre of the island. Across this road the rebels had erected their most formidable battery, with seemingly impenetrable swamps on either side, an ample space cleared for the play of their guns in front, and felled trees all around.

General Foster's brigade took the advance, having with it a battery of twelve-pounders from the fleet, to operate on the enemy's front. General Reno followed, with orders to penetrate on the left the frightful lagoons and thickets which protected the enemy's flank. A third column, under General Parke, brought up the rear.

General Foster rode forward with his staff into the woods, and made a reconnoissance. The line of pickets opened to let the brigade pass through. Not a drum was beat. Slowly, in silence, occasionally halting, regiment succeeded regiment, in perfect order, with heavy muffled tramp.

Along the forest road they passed, the men laughing and joking in high spirits, as if marching to a parade. The still, beautiful light of the innocent morning silvered the trees. The glistering branches arched above; the glistening stream of steel flowed beneath. Wreaths of vines, beards of moss, trailed their long fringes and graceful drapery from the boughs. The breeze shook down large shining drops, and every bush a soldier touched threw off its dancing shower.

"'And Ardennes waves above them her green leaves, dewy with nature's tear-drops, as they pass,'" remarked Seth Tucket.

"Come, none o' your solemncholy poetry to-day," said Jack Winch. "I never felt so jolly in my life.

There's only one kind of poetry I want to hear, and that's the pouring of our volleys into the rebels."

"The pouring of their volleys into us ain't quite so desirable, I suppose," said Harris.

"There wouldn't be much fun without some danger," said Jack.

"If that's fun, I guess Winch'll have fun enough before we're through with this job," remarked Ellis.

"What a long road it is!" cried Jack, impatiently.

"We'll come to a short turn in it pretty soon," said Atwater, significantly.

"Well, Abe has spoken!" said Jack. "His mouth has been shut so tight all along, I didn't think 'twould open till the time comes for him to cry quarter."

"Atwater means to let his gun speak for him to-day," said Harris.

"What do we go so slow for? Why don't we hurry on?" said Jack. "I want to get at the rebels some time this week. I don't believe they —— "

He was going to say that he didn't believe they would wait to fire a shot. But even as he spoke the confutation of his opinion resounded in the woods. Crack—crack—crack—went the rebel muskets; then followed a volley from the troops in advance.

"Why didn't you finish your sentence, Jack?" said Harris, with a smile.

"They're at it!" whispered Jack, in a changed voice.

"A little skirmishing," said Atwater, quietly.

Crack, crack, again; and — *sing!* — came a bullet over the heads of the men, cutting the leaves as it passed.

"Too high," laughed Gray, coolly.

"Halt!" come the command, which John Winch, for one, obeyed with amazing promptness.

"Hallo, Jack!" said Ellis; "who taught you to halt before the word is given?"

"Are they going to keep us standing here all day?" said Jack, presently.

"He's as wide awake now to be on the move as he was to stop," laughed Harris.

"Well," said Jack, nervously, "who likes to stand still and be shot at?"

"There's no shooting at us," replied Harris. "When it comes to that, we'll see the fun you talk about."

Fun! Jack's countenance looked like any thing but fun just then.

He gained some confidence by observing the officers coolly giving their orders, and the men coolly executing them, as if nothing of importance had happened, or was expected to happen.

Captain Edney deployed his company, pressing forward into the swamp. Bushes and fallen logs impeded their progress; the mud and water were in places leg-deep; and the men were permitted to pick their way as best they could. Suddenly out of a thicket a bullet came whizzing. Another and another followed. One tore the bark from a tree close by Captain Edney's head.

"Keep cool, boys!" he said; "and aim low."

He then gave the order, "Commence firing!" and the front rank men, halting, poured their volley into the thicket — their first shot at the enemy. Whilst they were reloading, the second rank advanced and delivered their fire.

"Don't waste a shot, my brave fellows!" cried the captain. "Fire wherever you see signs of a rebel. Always aim at *something*."

This last order was a very useful one; for many, in the excitement of coming for the first time under fire, were inclined to let off their pieces at random in the air; and the deliberation required to take aim, if only at a bush behind which a rebel might be concealed, had an excellent effect in quieting the nerves.

Yet some needed no such instruction. Atwater was observed to load and fire with as steady a hand and as serene a countenance as if he had been practising at a target. Others were equally calm and determined. There were some, however, even of the brave, who, from constitutional excitability, and not from any cowardice of spirit, exhibited symptoms of nervous-

ness.   Their cheeks paled and their hands shook.
But, the momentary tremor past, these men become
perhaps the most resolute and efficient of all.

Such a one was Frank; who, though in the rear
of the regiment, with the ambulance corps, felt his
heart beat so wildly at the first whiz of a bullet over
his head, that he was afraid he was going to be
afraid.

Was Jack Winch another of the sort? It was
pitiful to see him attempt to load his piece. He
never knew how it happened, but, instead of a cartridge, he got hold of the tompion, — called by the boys
the "tompin,"— used to stop the muzzle of the gun and
protect it from moisture, and was actually proceeding
to ram it down the barrel before he discovered his
mistake!

"Take a cartridge, Winch!" said Captain Edney,
who was coolly noting the conduct of his men.

So Jack, throwing away the stopper, took a cartridge. But his hand shook *around* the muzzle of
the gun so that it was some time before he could
insert the charge. He had already dodged behind a
tree, the men being allowed to shelter themselves
when they could.

"Dry ground is scarce as hens' teeth!" remarked
Seth Tucket, droll as ever, looking for a good place
to stand while he was loading.

"Fun, ain't it?" said Ned Ellis, who had sought cover by the same tree with Winch.

He stood at Jack's left hand, and a little behind him. Jack, too much agitated to respond to the unseasonable jest, threw up the barrel of his piece, in order to prime, when a bullet came, from nobody knew where, aslant, and put an end to jesting for the present.

Jack felt a benumbing shock, and dropped his gun, the stock of which had been shivered in his grasp. At the same instant Ellis dropped his gun also, and threw out his hands wildly, exclaiming, —

"I am shot!"

And both fell to the ground together.

"That's what ye call two birds with one stun!" said Tucket, a flash of ferocity kindling his face as he saw his comrades fall. "Pay 'em for that, boys! Pay 'em for that!"

And hearing the order to charge the thicket, he went forward with a yell, taking strides that would have done credit to a moose in his own native woods of Maine.

Ellis had by this time got upon his feet again. But Jack lay still, his neck bathed in blood.

XXVIII.

JACK WINCH'S CATASTROPHE.

SEVERAL companies were by this time engaged driving in the rebel skirmishers, and three or four men had been disabled.

It was impracticable to take the stretchers, or litters for the wounded, into such a wilderness of bogs and thickets; and accordingly the most forward and courageous of the carriers leaped into the swamps without them.

As soon as Frank heard that some of his company had been wounded, all sense of danger to himself was forgotten, and no remonstrance from his friend the drum-major could prevent his rushing in to assist in bringing them off.

Finding that the boy, whose welfare was so precious to him, could not be restrained, Mr. Sinjin plunged in with him, and kept at his side, scrambling through mud and brush and water, and over logs and roots, in the direction of the firing.

They had not gone far when they met a wounded

soldier coming out. His right hand hung mangled and ghastly and bleeding at his side. A slug from a rifled musket had ploughed it through, nearly severing the fingers from the wrist.

"Ellis!" cried Frank — "you hurt?"

Ned swung the disabled and red-dripping member up to view, with a sorry smile.

"Not so bad as might be!" he said, with a rather faint show of gayety. "Jack has got it worse."

"Jack who?" — for there were several Jacks in the company.

"Winch," said Ellis, whilst the old drummer was binding up his hand to stop the blood.

"Is he killed?" asked Frank, with a strange feeling — almost of remorse, remembering his late bitter and vindictive thoughts towards John.

"I don't know. We were both hit by the same ball, I believe. It must have passed through his neck. It came from one side, and we tumbled both together. What I tumbled for, I don't know. It didn't take me long to pick myself up again!"

"And Jack?"

"There he lies, with blood all over his face."

"And nobody caring for him?"

"The boys have something else to think of!" said Ellis, with a pallid smile.

Mr. Sinjin, having tied up the wound, directed him

18

how to find the surgeon. And Ellis, in return, pointed out the best way to get at Jack.

The company had advanced, driving the rebel skirmishers before them, and leaving Winch where he had fallen. Frank and his companion soon reached the spot. There lay the hapless youth under the roots of the tree, the left side of his face and neck all covered with gore.

"Jack!" cried Frank, stooping by his side, and lifting his arm.

No answer. The arm fell heavily again as he released it.

"Dead!" said the boy, a sudden calmness coming over him. "We may as well leave him where he is, and look for others."

"Not dead yet," said the more experienced Sinjin, feeling Jack's heart, which was beating still. In corroboration of which statement Winch uttered something between a gasp and a groan, and rolled up horrible eyes.

Frank was standing, and the old man was trying to find Winch's wound, in order to prevent his bleeding to death while they were carrying him out, when the report of a rifle sounded, seemingly quite near, and a bullet passed with a swift vehement buzz close by their ears. At the instant Frank felt something like a quick tap or jerk on his arm. He looked, and saw that the strip of red flannel, which betokened the service he was engaged in, and which should have rendered his person sacred from any intentional harm, had been shot away. A hole had been torn in his sleeve also, but his flesh was untouched.

The old drummer looked up quickly.

"Are you hurt?"

"No," said Frank, feeling of his arm while he looked around to discover where the shot came from. "It must have been a spent ball; for, see! it fell there in the water!"—pointing at a pool behind them, the surface of which was still rippling with the plunge of the shot.

Winch gave another groan.

"The wound must be an internal one," said Sinjin, "for he is not bleeding much now."

Frank assisted to lift him, and together they bore him back towards the road. It was a difficult task. Frank had neither the stature nor the strength of a man; but he made up in energy and good will what he lacked in force. Very carefully, very tenderly, through bogs and through thickets, they carried the helpless, heavy weight of the blood-stained volunteer.

"Frank! is it you?" murmured Winch, faintly.

"Yes, Jack!" panted the boy, out of breath with exertion.

"Am I killed?" articulated Jack.

"O, no!" said Frank. "You've got a bullet in you somewhere; but I guess the surgeon will soon have it out, and you'll be all right again."

"O!" groaned Jack.

Just then there came another rifle-crack, not quite so near as before, and another bullet came with its angry buzz. It cut a twig just over Mr. Sinjin's head, and grazed a cypress tree farther on, at a point considerably lower, and with a downward slant, as the mark revealed.

"Another spent ball," said Frank.

But the old drummer shook his head. "Those are no spent balls. Some murderous rebel is aiming at us."

"How can that be?"

"I don't know. And our best way is not to stop to inquire, but to get out of this as soon as possible."

"Frank!" groaned the burden they were bearing.

"What, Jack?"

"Forgive me, Frank!"

"For what?" said Frank, cheerily.

"For writing home lies about you."

"They were not all lies, I'm sorry to say, Jack. But even if they were, I forgive you from my very soul."

Jack groaned, and said no more. Assistants now came to meet them, and Frank, who was almost exhausted with the fatigue of bringing his comrade so far, was relieved of the burden. The road was near, and Jack was soon laid upon a stretcher.

"Frank!" he gasped, rolling his eyes again, "don't leave me! For God's sake, stay by me, Frank!"

So Frank kept by his side, while the men bore him along the road to a tree, where the surgeon had hung up his red flag, and established his hospital.

Ellis had just undergone the amputation of his mangled hand, without once flinching under the surgeon's knife, and he remained on the spot to encourage Winch.

"If I die," began Jack, stirring himself more than he had been observed to do before. "Frank, do you hear me?"

"What is it, Jack?" asked the sympathizing boy.

"If I die, don't let me be buried on this miserable island!"

"But you are not going to die," said the surgeon, kindly, cutting away the clothes from his neck.

Mr. Singin assisted, while Frank anxiously awaited the result of the examination. The surgeon looked puzzled. There was blood, but not any fresh blood — and no wound! Not so much as a scratch of the skin.

Jack in the mean time was groaning dismally.

"What are you making that noise for?" exclaimed

the surgeon, sharply. "There isn't a hurt about you!"

"Ain't I shot?" cried Jack, starting up, as much astonished as any body; for he had really believed he was a dead man. "I was hit, I know! and I swooned away."

"You swooned from fright, then," declared the indignant surgeon. "Take the fellow away!"

Jack, however, gratified as he was to learn he was not killed, testily insisted that a bullet had passed through him, adducing the blood on his face as a proof.

Thereupon Ellis broke into a laugh.

"It takes Jack to make capital out of a little borrowed blood. I know something about that. When my hand was ploughed through, I slapped it against his face; and down he went, fainting dead away." And, notwithstanding the ache of his wound and his weakness, and the scenes of horror thickening around, Ned leaned back against the tree, and laughed merrily at what he called Jack's "awful big scare."

Frank felt immensely relieved, at first, on learning that Jack was not killed; then immensely amused; and, lastly, immensely disgusted. He remembered the severe struggle it cost to bring him out of the swamp, the rolled-up eyes, the lugubrious groans, and the faintly murmured dying request to be forgiven.

And in the revulsion of his feelings he could not help saying, "Yes, Jack, I forgive ye! and if you die, you shan't be buried on this miserable island."

He was excited when he uttered this taunt, and he was sorry for it afterwards. Seeing the craven slink away, conscious of the scorn of every body, he felt a touch of pity for him.

"Jack," said he, with friendly intent, "why don't you go back and wipe out this disgrace? *I* would."

"Because," snarled Jack, goaded by his own shame and the general contempt, "I'm hurt, I tell ye! *internally*, I s'pose," — for he had heard Mr. Sinjin use the word, and thought it a good one to suit his case. And he lay down wretchedly by the roadside, and counterfeited anguish, while the fresh troops marched by to the battle.

A fiery impulse seized the drummer boy. He glanced at his torn sleeve, from which the badge had been shot away, and thought there was something besides accident in what appeared so much like an omen. If it meant any thing, was it not that his place was elsewhere than in the ambulance corps?

He turned to Mr. Sinjin, and asked to þe excused from going with the stretcher. And Mr. Sinjin, who prized the boy's safety too highly to wish to see him go again under fire, was only too glad to excuse him, never once suspecting what wild purpose was in his heart.

The battle was now fairly begun. The rebel battery had opened. The continual rattle of musketry and the thunder of heavy cannon shook the island. The regiments in line in front of the cleared space before the battery, returned the fire with energy, and the marine howitzers also responded. Soon a shell from the enemy's work came flying through the woods with a hum, which increased to a howl, and burst with a startling explosion within a few rods of the hospital. Nobody was hurt; but the incident had a very marked effect on Jack Winch. He got better at once, and moved to the rear with an alacrity surprisingly in contrast with his recent helplessness.

XXIX.

HOW FRANK GOT NEWS OF HIS BROTHER.

FRANK was already moving off quite as rapidly, but in the opposite direction. He plunged once more into the swamp, and returned to the spot where Jack had fallen. The battle was raging beyond; the troops had passed on; the ground was deserted. But there lay Winch's gun; with his cartridge-box beside it. Near by was Ellis's piece, abandoned where it had fallen. There, too, lay the red badge which had been shot from Frank's arm. He picked it up, thinking his mother would like to have him preserve it.

Then he slipped on the cartridge-box, and took up Winch's gun; for this was the resolution which inspired him — to assume the poltroon's place in the company, and by his own conduct to atone for the disgrace he had brought upon it.

But the gun-stock was, as has been said, shattered; and Frank could not have the satisfaction of revenging himself and his comrades for Winch's cowardice

(281)

with Winch's own gun. So he threw it down, and took up Ellis's, which he found ready loaded and primed.

While he was examining the piece, he remembered the shots which he had taken for spent balls, and bethought him to look around the woods in the direction from which they had come. Raising his eyes above the undergrowth, he beheld a singular phenomenon.

At first, he thought it was a wild animal — a coon, or a wildcat, coming down a tree. Then there were two wildcats, descending together, or preparing to descend. Then the wildcats became two human legs clasped around the trunk, and two human arms appeared enjoying an equally close hug above them. The body to which these visible members appertained was itself invisible, being on the farther side of the trunk.

"That's the chap that was shooting at us!" was Frank's instantaneous conviction.

And now he could plainly discern an object slung across the man's back, as his movements swung it around a little to one side. It was the sharpshooter's rifle.

Frank was so excited that he felt himself trembling — not with fear, but with the very ardor of his ambition.

"Since he has had two shots at me, why shouldn't I have as much as one at him?"

To disable and bring in the rebel who had shot the badge from his arm — what a triumph!

But he was not in a good position for an effective shot, even if he could have made up his mind to fire at a person who, though without doubt an enemy, was not at the moment defending himself. It seemed, after all, too dreadful a thing deliberately to kill a man.

Frank's excitement did not embarrass his faculties in the least, but only rendered them all the more keenly alive and vigilant. It took him but a moment to decide what to do. Through the swamp he ran with a lightness and agility of which in calmer moments he would have been scarcely capable. The exigency of the occasion inspired him. Such leaps he took over miry places! so safely and swiftly he ran the length of an old mossy log! so nimbly he avoided the undergrowth! and so suddenly he arrived at last at the tree the rebel was descending!

For he was a rebel indeed. Frank knew that by his gray uniform and short jacket. He had been perched in the thick top of a tall pine to pick off our men during the skirmish. It was he who had taken the bark from the tree near Captain Edney's head. It was he who had basely thought to assassinate those who were carrying away the wounded. And now, the advancing troops having passed him, he was taking advantage of the solitary situation to slip down the trunk and make his escape through the woods.

Unfortunately for him, he could not go up and down trees like a squirrel. He proceeded *hugging* his way so slowly and laboriously that Frank reached the spot when he was still within a dozen feet of the ground. Hearing a noise, and looking down over his arm, and seeing Frank, he would have jumped the remainder of the distance. But Frank was prepared for that.

" Stop, or I'll fire ! "

Shrill and menacing rang the boy's determined tones through the soul of the treed rebel. He saw the gun pointed up at him ; so he stopped.

" What's wanting ? " said he, gruffly.

" I want you to throw down that rifle as quick as ever you can ! " cried Frank.

" What do you want of my rifle ? "

" I've a curiosity to see what sort of a piece you use to shoot at men carrying off the wounded."

And the " grayback " (as the boys termed the rebels) could hear the ominous click of the gun-lock in Frank's hands.

" Was it you I fired at ? "

"Yes, it was; and I'm bound to put lead into you now, if you don't do as I tell you pretty quick!"

"I can't throw my gun down; I can't get it off," remonstrated the man.

"You never will come down from that tree alive, unless you do!" said Frank.

"Well, take the d——d thing then!" growled the man. And unclasping one arm from the tree, while he held on with the other and his two legs, he slipped the belt over his head, and dropped the gun to the ground. "If it had been good for any thing, I reckon you wouldn't be here now, bothering me!" he added, significantly.

"No doubt!" said Frank. "You are brave fellows, to shoot out of trees at men carrying off the wounded. Wait! I'm not quite ready for you yet."

And he stood under the tree, with his musket pointed upwards, ready cocked, and with the point of the bayonet in rather ticklish proximity to the most exposed and prominent part of the rebel's person.

"Ye think I'm going to stick here all day?" growled the desperate climber.

"You'll stick there till you throw me down your revolver," Frank resolutely informed him.

"How do you know I've got a revolver?"

"1 saw your hand make a motion at your pocket.

You thought you'd try a shot at me. But you saw at the very next motion you'd be a dead man!"

"You mean to say you'd blow my brains out?"

"Yes, if your brains are where my gun is aimed, as I think the brains of rebels must be, or they never would have seceded."

Frank's gun, by the way, was aimed at the above mentioned very exposed and prominent part.

"Grayback" grinned and growled.

"Come, my young joker, I can't stand this!"

"You'll have to stand it till you throw down that revolver!"

"I'm slipping!"

"Then I'll give you something sharp to slip on!"

The man felt that he had really betrayed himself by making the involuntary movement towards his breast-pocket, which Frank had been too shrewd not to notice. The cocked gun, and bayonet, and resolute young face below, were inexorable. So he yielded.

"Don't throw it towards me! Drop it the other side!" cried the wary Frank.

The revolver was tossed down. Then Frank stepped back, and let the man descend from his uncomfortable position.

"Boy!" said the man, as soon as his feet were safe on the ground, and he could turn to look at his captor, "I reckon you're a cute 'un! A Yankee, ain't ye?"

"Yes, and proud to own it!" said Frank. "Keep your distance!"—as the man made a move to come nearer—"and don't you stoop to touch that gun!"

"Look here," said the man, coaxingly, "you'd better let me go! I'm out of ammunition, and can't hurt anybody. I'll give ye ten dollars if you will."

"In confederate shinplasters?"

The rebel laughed. "No, in Uncle Sam's gold."

"You don't place a very high value on yourself," said Frank. "You are too modest."

"Twenty dollars!"—jingling the money in his pocket. "Come, I'm a gentleman at home, and I don't want to go north. Well, say thirty dollars."

"If you hadn't said you were a gentleman, I might trade," said Frank. "But a gentleman is worth more than you bid. You wouldn't insult a negro by offering that for him!"

"Fifty dollars, then! I see you are sharp at a bargain. And you shall keep that revolver."

"I intend to keep this, any way," said Frank, picking it up. "And the gun that shot at me, too," slinging it on his back.

The rebel, seeing his determination, rose in his bids at once to a hundred dollars.

"Not for a hundred thousand!" said Frank, who was now ready to move his prisoner. "You are going the way my bayonet points, and no other. March!"

The rebel marched accordingly.

Frank followed at a distance of two or three paces, prepared at any moment to use prompt measures in case his prisoner should attempt to turn upon him or make his escape.

"How many of you fellows are hid around in these trees?" said Frank.

"Not many just around here — lucky for you!" muttered the disconsolate rebel.

"Is that your favorite way of fighting?"

"People fight any way they can when their soil is invaded."

"What are holes cut in the pine trees for, — footholds for climbing?"

"Holes? them's turpentine boxes!" said the man, in some surprise at Frank's ignorance. "Didn't you ever see turpentine boxes before?"

"Never till last evening. Is that the way you get turpentine?"

"That's the way we get turpentine. The sap begins to run and fill the boxes along in March, and when they are full we dip it out with ladles made on purpose, and put it into barrels."

"O, you needn't stop to explain!" cried Frank. "Push ahead!"

And the rebel pushed ahead.

It was a moment of unspeakable satisfaction to the

drummer boy when he had brought his prisoner
through all the difficulties of the way to the road.
There he had him safe.

He was now in the midst of shocking and terrible
scenes, but he heeded them not as much as he would
have heeded the smallest accident to a fellow-creature
a few hours before. Already he seemed familiar with
battles and all their horrors. Men were hurrying by
with medical stores. The wounded were passing, on
stretchers, or in the arms of their friends, or limping
painfully, ghastly, bleeding, but heroic still. They
smiled as they showed their frightful hurts. One
poor fellow had had his arm torn off by a cannon
ball: the flesh hung in strings. Some lay by the
roadside, faint from the loss of blood. And all the
time the deadly, deafening tumult of the battle
went on.

To guard his prisoner securely was Frank's first
thought. But greater, more absorbing even than that,
was the wild wish to see the enemies of his country
defeated, and to share in the glorious victory.

"Frank Manly! what sort of a beast have you got
there?" cried a soldier, returning from the action
with a slight wound.

Frank recognized a member of another company
in the same regiment to which he belonged.

"I've got a sharpshooter that I've taken prisoner."

19

And he briefly related his adventure, every word of which the rebel, who rather admired his youthful captor, voluntarily confirmed.

"It's just as he tells you," he said, assuming a candid, reckless air. "I am well enough satisfied. If your men are equal to your boys, I shall have plenty of company before night."

"You think we shall have you all prisoners?" inquired Frank, eagerly.

"This island," replied the rebel, "is a perfect trap. I've known it from the beginning. You outnumber us two to one, and if the fight goes against us, we've no possible chance of escape. We've five thousand men on the island, and if we're whipped you'll make a pretty respectable bag. But you never can conquer us," — he hastened to add, fearing lest he was conceding too much.

"Can't, eh?" laughed Frank. "Where's the last ditch?"

"Never mind about that," said the prisoner, with a peculiar grin.

By this time several other stragglers had gathered around them, eager to hear the story of the drummer boy's exploit.

The rebel had looked curiously at his youthful captor ever since he had heard him called by name. At length he said: —

"Have you got a brother in the confederate army?"

Frank changed color. "Why do you ask that?"

"Because we have a Captain Manly, from the north somewhere, who looks enough like you to be a pretty near relation."

Frank trembled with interest as he inquired, "What is his given name?"

"Captain — Captain *George* Manly, I'm pretty sure."

"Yes, sir," — and sorry tears came into Frank's eyes as he spoke, — "I suppose I must own he is my brother."

"Well, you've a smart chance of meeting him, I reckon, — if, as I said, your men are equal to your boys. For he's fighting against you to-day, and he's one of the pluckiest, and he won't run."

XXX.

THE BOYS MEET AN OLD ACQUAINTANCE.

Frank was anxious to inquire further concerning his apostate brother; but at this moment one of Foster's aids came up, and saw the prisoner.

"Where did you find that fellow?" The story was quickly told. "Well," said the officer, "you've taken the first prisoner to-day."

He then turned to question the captive, who seemed inclined to talk freely about the position and force of the confederates.

"I'll take this fellow in charge," he said, perceiving that it was in his power to give valuable information. "Come too, if you like."

"I thank you; I want to join my company," said Frank.

"You'd rather do that than come and see the general?"

"I can see him any time when he wants me, but we don't have a fight every day, sir."

"Well, he shall hear of you. Can I do any thing for you?" (292)

"If you please, you may take this gun that I have captured; one is enough for me."

The officer took it, saying, as he turned to go, —

"A spirited boy, and as modest as he is brave!"

In the mean time Frank's comrades in the fight were cutting their way through a thick swampy jungle in the direction of the enemy's left flank.

Relieved of his prisoner, his ardor inflamed rather than quenched by the evil tidings he had heard of his brother, he followed in their track, passing directly across the fire of the battery.

The hurricane of destruction swept howling over him. The atmosphere was thick with smoke. Grape-shot whizzed through the bushes. The scream of rifled shot seemed to fill the very air with terror and shuddering. Right before him a shell struck a forest tree, shivering limbs and trunk in an instant, as if a bolt from heaven had fallen upon it. He felt that at any moment his tender body too might be torn in pieces; but he believed God's arm was about him, and that he would be preserved. Deep and solemn, happy even, was that conviction. A sense of the grand and terrible filled him; the whole soul of the boy was roused. He was not afraid of any thing. He felt ready for any thing, even death, in his country's service.

The mud was deep, and savage the entanglement

of bushes on every side. But the troops, breaking through, had made the way comparatively easy to follow, and Frank soon overtook the regiment.

Great was Captain Edney's surprise at sight of him, with a gun in his hand and with the glow of youthful heroism in his face.

" What are you here for ? "

" To beg permission to take Winch's place in the ranks."

" Your place is with the ambulance corps."

" I got excused from that, sir. I am not strong enough to carry heavy men through the swamps," said Frank, with a smile.

"But strong enough to take a man's place in the ranks !" said Captain Edney.

"I would like to have you try me, sir."

You may know that Captain Edney loved the boy to whom he gave so many words and such serious thought at a time of action and peril. Perhaps he had heard of Winch's pusillanimity, and understood the spirit which prompted Frank to fill his place. Certain it is he saw in the lad's eye the guarantee that, if permitted, he would give no cowardly account of himself that day. So, reluctantly, dreading lest evil might happen to him, he granted his request; and with a thrill of joy, Frank sprang to Atwater's side.

"I'm here, old Abe!"

"I'm glad — and sorry!" said Abe.

The company had halted, awaiting the movement of the troops in front.

"We are getting into a splendid position!" said Gray, who had passed through the undergrowth to reconnoitre. "We're fairly on their flank, and not discovered yet!"

"How far did you go?" asked Captain Edney.

"To the clearing, which is just there where the woods look lighter. I could see the guns of the battery blazing away, and rebels in the woods supporting it. They're too busy to notice us."

"We're discovered, though!" said Captain Edney as a bullet came chipping its way among the twigs above them.

"The sharpshooters are after us!" said Gray, gayly. "And now we're after them!"

The order was given to advance. The men dashed forward through the bushes. They soon made the clearing, and marching along its edge, opened fire by file upon the battery and the rebels in the woods.

"You do well, Frank!" said Atwater, seeing his young companion coolly loading and firing at his side.

"It's a perfect surprise to them! they didn't think we could do it!" cried Gray, elated. "Lively, boys! lively!"

The firing, regular at first, running along the line from right to left, soon became a continual rattling, each man loading at will, and firing whenever an enemy's head showed itself.

"There! I popped you over, you sneaking rebel!" cried Seth Tucket, watching the effect of his shot. "Take the fellow next to him there, Harris! behind that stump!"

"Let him put up his head a little higher!" said Harris, taking aim.

He fired. The rebel dropped, not behind the stump, but beside it.

"You've saved him!" shouted Tucket. "That'll pay for Ellis and Jack Winch!"

The fire of the enemy in the woods was soon concentrated on Captain Edney's company, which happened to be most exposed.

"Fire and load lying!" rang the captain's voice through the din.

Frank saw those next him throw themselves down behind a fallen tree. He did the same. The trunk presented an excellent rest for his musket, and he fired across it. But when he came to load, he found difficulty. He had been exercised in the manual of arms, yet the operation of ramming the cartridge while on his back was beyond his practice. Give him time, and he could do it. But he felt that time was precious, and that every shot told.

He glanced at Atwater, resting on his left side as he brought his gun back after discharging it; taking out his cartridge; then turning on his back, holding the piece with both hands and placing the butt between his feet; and in that position, with the barrel over his breast, charging cartridge, drawing rammer, and so forth.

All which the tall soldier performed scientifically and quickly. Yet Frank saw that it took even him much longer to load lying than standing. What, then, could he hope to do?

What he did was this. He deliberately got upon his feet, and with the balls singing around him, proceeded unconcernedly with his loading.

"Down!" called Atwater to him; "down! You're making a target of yourself!"

Frank resolutely went on with his loading.

"Down, there! down, Frank!" shouted Captain Edney.

Frank shouted back, —

"I can't load unless I stand up, sir!"

"Never mind that! Down!" repeated his captain, peremptorily.

"I've got my cartridge down, any way," said Frank, triumphantly, dropping again behind the log.

"Why don't you obey orders?" cried Gray.

"The orders were to load and fire, and I was bound

to obey them before any others!" said Frank, preparing to prime.

Just then Atwater, who was again on his back, suddenly dropped his piece, which fell across his left arm, and brought his right hand to his breast. The movement was so abrupt and unusual it attracted Frank's attention.

"Are you hit, Abe?"

And in an instant he saw the answer to his hurried question in a gush of blood which crimsoned the poor, brave fellow's breast.

"It has come!" said Atwater.

"How could it — and you lying down so!" ejaculated Frank.

"I don't know — never mind me!" replied Abe, faintly.

Then Frank remembered the mysterious shots aimed at him and Sinjin in the woods, and the subsequent solution of the mystery. He looked up — all around — overhead.

"What's the trouble, Manly?" screamed Tucket. "What do ye see?"

"There!" Frank shouted, pointing upwards; "there! the man that killed Atwater!"

And in the branches of a tree, which stood but a few paces in front of them, he showed, half hidden by the thick masses, the figure of a rebel.

The sharpshooter was loading his piece. Frank saw
the movement, and would have hastened to avenge
the death of his friend before the assassin could fire
again. But he was out of caps, and must borrow.
Tucket's gun was ready.

"'Die thou shalt, gray-headed ruffian!'"

Seth shouted the words up at the man in the tree,
and lying on his back, brought the butt of his gun to
his shoulder, aimed heavenward, and fired.

Scarce had flame shot from the muzzle, when down
came the rebel's gun tumbling to the ground; pursued
out of the tree by something that resembled a huge
bird, with spread wings, swooping down terribly, and
striking the ground with a jar heard even amid the
thunder of battle.

It was the rebel himself.

"'Rattling, crashing, thrashing, thunder down!'"
screamed Seth Tucket, his ruling passion, poetry,
strong even in battle.

The man, pitching forwards in his fearful somerset,
had fallen within a few feet of Frank. The boy, recovering from his astonishment at the awful sight, felt
a strange curiosity to see if he was dead.

He looked over the log. There lay the wretch, a
hideous heap, the face of him upturned and recogniz-
able.

Where had Frank seen that grim countenance, that

short, stiff, iron-gray hair? Somewhere, surely. He looked again, trying to fix his memory.

"I swan to man, ef it ain't old Buckley!"

Seth was right. It was the Maryland secessionist whose turkeys the boys had stolen, and who, in consequence, had made haste to avenge his wrongs by joining the confederate army.

A strange, sickening sensation came over Frank at the discovery. Thus the evil he had done followed him. But for that wild freak of plundering the poor man's poultry-yard, he might be plodding now on his Maryland farm, and Atwater would not be lying there so white and still with a bullet in his breast.

XXXI.

"VICTORY OR DEATH."

WHERE all this time was the old drum-major? He too had disappeared from the ambulance corps, to assume, like Frank, a position of still more arduous service and greater danger.

Shortly after Frank left him, word came that the battery of boat-howitzers, which, from a curve in the road that commanded the rebel works, had been doing splendid execution, was suffering terribly, and getting short of hands. It must soon withdraw unless reënforced. But who would volunteer to help work the guns?

The old man had been familiar with artillery practice. At the thought of the service and the peril his spirit grew proud within him. But his heart yearned for Frank.

"Where is Manly?" he inquired of Ellis.

"I believe he has gone into the fight with our company," said the wounded volunteer.

The truth flashed upon the veteran. Yes, the boy

he loved had gone before him into danger. He no longer hesitated, or lost any time in getting leave to report himself to the commander of the battery.

"What can you do?" was the hurried question put to him, as he stood in the thick powder-smoke, calmly asking for work.

Just then, a gunner was taken off his feet by a cannon-ball.

"I can take this fellow's place, sir," said the old man, grimly.

"Take it!" replied the officer.

The wounded sailor was borne away, and the old drummer, springing to the howitzer, assisted in working it until, its ammunition exhausted, the battery was ordered to withdraw.

During the severest part of the action Mr. Sinjin had observed a person in citizen's dress, with his coat off, briskly handling the cannon-balls. Their work done, he turned to speak with him.

"You are a friend of my young drummer boy, I believe," said the old man.

"Yes, and a friend of all his friends!" cordially answered the white-sleeved civilian.

"You can preach well, and fight well," said the veteran, his eyes gleaming with stern pride.

"I prefer to preach, but I believe in fighting too, when duty points that way," said Mr. Egglestone, —

for it was he, flushed and begrimed with his toil at the deadly guns.

Even as they were speaking, a cannon-ball passed between them. Mr. Egglestone was thrown back by the shock of the wind it carried, but recovered instantly to find himself unhurt. But where was the old drummer? He was not there. And it was some seconds before the bewildered clergyman perceived him, several paces distant, lying on his face by the road.

The howitzers silenced, it was determined to storm the enemy's works.

Frank afterwards had the satisfaction of knowing that it was in part the information gained from the prisoner he had taken that decided the commanding general to order a charge.

Frank was with his company, where we left him, when suddenly yells rent the air; and, looking, he saw the Zouaves of Parke's brigade dashing down the causeway in front of the rebel redoubt.

They were met by a murderous fire. They returned it as they charged. As their comrades fell, they passed over them unheedingly, and still kept on — a sublime sight to look upon, in their wild Arab costumes, shouting, "Zou! zou!" bounding like tigers, clearing obstructions, and sweeping straight to the breastwork with their deadly bayonets.

"What is it?" asked Atwater, faintly.

"Victory!" answered Frank; for the firing ceased — the enemy were flying.

"That's enough!" And the still pallid face of the soldier smiled.

Victory! None but those who have fought a stern foe to the bloody close, and seen his ranks break and fly, and the charging columns pursue, ranks of bristling steel rushing in through clouds of battle smoke, know what pride and exultation are in that word.

Victory! Reno's column, that had outflanked the rebels on the west side, fighting valiantly, charged simultaneously with the Zouaves. The whole line followed the example, and went in with colors flying, and shouts of joy filling the welkin which had been shaken so lately with the jar of battle. Over fallen trees, over pits and ditches, through brush, and bog, and water, the conquering hosts poured in; Frank's regiment with the rest, and himself among the foremost that planted their standard on the breastwork.

There were the abandoned cannon, still warm and smoking. There lay a deserted flag, bearing the Latin inscription "*Aut vincere aut mori*," — Victory or death, — flung down in the precipitate flight.

"They couldn't conquer, and they didn't want to die; so they split the difference, and run," observed Seth Tucket.

There too lay the dead and dying, whom the boast-

ful enemy had forsaken where they fell. One of these
who had *not* run was an officer — handsome and
young. He was not yet dead. A strange light was
in his eyes as he looked on the forms of the foemen
thronging around him, saw the faces of the victors,
and heard the cheering. Success and glory were for
them — for him defeat and death.

"Lift me up," he said, "and let me look at you
once."

They raised him to a sitting posture, supported
partly by a gun-carriage, and partly by the arms of
his conquerors. And they pressed around him, their
voices hushed, their triumphant brows saddened with
respect for the dying.

"Though we have been fighting each other," he
said, solemnly, "we are still brothers. God forgive
me if I have done wrong! I too am a northern man,
— I too —— "

As he spoke, a figure in the uniform of his foes
sprang through the crowd to his feet.

"O, my brother! O, my brother George!"

It was Frank Manly, who knelt, and with passionate grief clasped the hand that had clasped his in
fondness and merry sport so often in the happy days
of his childhood, when neither ever dreamed of their
unnatural separation and this still more unnatural
meeting.

20

"Frank! my little brother! so grown! is it you?" said the wounded captive, with dreamy surprise.

"O George! how could you?" Frank began, with anguish in his voice. But he checked himself; he would not reproach his dying brother.

"My wife, you know!" was all the unhappy young man could murmur. He looked at Frank with a faint and ever fainter smile of love, till his eyes grew dim. "I am going, Frank. It is all wrong — I know now — but it is too late. Tell mother —— "

His words became inaudible, and he sank, swooning, in Captain Edney's arms.

"What, George? what shall I tell mother?" pleaded Frank, in an agony.

"And father too," said the dying lips, in a moment of reviving recollection. "And my sisters —— " But the message was never uttered.

"George! O, George! I am here! Don't you see me?"

The dim eyes opened; but they saw not.

"Carry me up stairs! Let me die in the old room — our room, Frank."

It was evident his mind was wandering; he fancied himself once more at home, and wished to be laid in the little chamber where he used to sleep with Frank, as Frank had slept with Willie in later days.

"Kiss me, mother!" The ashen face smiled; then

the light faded from it; and the lips, grown cold and numb, murmured softly, "It is growing dark —— Good night!"

And he slept — the sleep of eternity.

When Frank rose up from the corpse he had mastered himself. Then Captain Edney saw, what none had noticed before, that blood was streaming down his arm — the same arm that had been grazed before; this time it had been shot through.

" You are wounded ! "

" Yes — but not much. I must go — let me go and take care of Atwater ! "

" But you need taking care of yourself! " — for he was deadly pale.

" No, sir — I — Abe, there —— "

Even as the boy was speaking he grew dizzy, and fell fainting in his captain's arms.

XXXII.

AFTER THE BATTLE.

It is over. The battle is ended, the victory won. The sun goes down upon conquerors and conquered, upon the living and the dead. And the evening comes, melancholy. The winds sigh in the pine-tops, the sullen waves dash upon the shore, the gloom of the cypresses lies dismal and dark on Roanoke Island.

Buildings suitable for the purpose, taken from the enemy, have been converted into hospitals, and the wounded are brought in.

There is Frank with his bandaged arm, and Ellis with his stump of a hand bound up, and others worse off than they. There is the surgeon of their regiment, active, skilful, kind. There, too, is Mr. Egglestone, the minister, proving his claim to that high title, ministering in the truest sense to all who need him, holding to fevered lips the cup of medicine or soothing drink, and holding to fevered souls the still more precious drink.

There is Corporal Gray, assisting to arrange the

nospital, and cheering his comrades with an account of the victory.

"The rebels ran like herds of deer after we got the battery. We tracked 'em by the traps they threw away. Guns, knapsacks, coats, — they flung off every thing, and skedaddled for dear life! We met an old negro woman, who told us where their camp was; but some of 'em had taken another direction, by a road that goes to the east side of the island. Our boys followed, and found 'em embarking in boats. We fired on 'em, and brought back two of their boats. In one we got Jennings Wise, of the Wise Legion, that we had the bloody fight with flanking the battery. He was wounded and dying.

"But our greatest haul was the camp the old negress pointed out. The rebels rallied, and as we moved up, fired upon us, doing no damage. We returned the compliment, and dropped eight men. Then more running, of the same chivalrous sort, our boys after them; when out comes a flag of truce from the camp.

"'What terms will be granted us?' says the rebel officer.

"'No terms, but unconditional surrender,' says General Foster.

"'How long a time will be granted us to consider?'

"'Just time enough for you to go to your camp to convey the terms, and return.'

"Off went the rebel. We waited fifteen minutes. Then we pushed on again. That movement quickened their deliberations; and out came Colonel Shaw, the commander, and says to General Foster, —

"'I give up my sword, and surrender five thousand men!' For he didn't know some two thousand of his force had escaped. What we have got is about three thousand prisoners, and all their forts and quarters, which we call a pretty good bag."

The boys forgot their wounds, they forgot their dead and dying comrades, listening to this recital. But short-lived was the enthusiasm of one, at least. Scarce was Gray gone, when Frank saw four men enter with a stretcher, bringing upon it a grizzled, pallid old man.

"O, Mr. Sinjin! O, my dear, dear friend! You too!"

"Is it my boy?" said the veteran, with a wan smile. "Yes, I too! They have done for me, I fear."

"But nobody told me. How — where —— " The boy's grief choked his voice.

"An impertinent cannon-ball interrupted my conversation with Mr. Egglestone," said the old man, stifling his agony as the men removed him to a cot. "And took a — " he groaned in spite of himself — " a greedy mouthful out of my side — that's all."

Frank knew not what to say or what to do, he was so overcome.

" There, my boy," said the old man, to comfort him,
" no tears for me! It is enough to see you again.
They told me you were hurt —" looking at the lad's
disabled arm. " I am glad it is no worse." And the
wan veteran smiled content.

Frank, with his one hand, smoothed the pillow
under the old gray head, struggling hard to keep
back his sobs as he did so.

" Who is my neighbor there?" Mr. Sinjin cheerfully asked.

"Atwater," Frank managed to articulate.

" Is it? I am sorry! A bad wound?"

" The bullet went through a Bible he carried,
then into his breast, beyond the reach of surgery, I
am afraid," Mr. Egglestone answered for Frank.
"He lies in a stupor, just alive."

" Poor fellow!" said Mr. Sinjin, feelingly. " If
Death must have one of us, let him for once be con-
siderate, and take me. Atwater is young, just married, — he needs to live; but I — I am not of much
account to any body, and can just as well be spared
as not."

" O, no, O, no!" sobbed Frank; " I can't spare you!
I can't let you die!"

" My boy," said the old man, deeply affected, " I
would like to tarry a little longer in the world, if only
for your sake. You have done so much for me — so

much more than you can ever know! You have
brought back to my old heart more of its youth and
freshness than it had felt for years. I thank God for
it. I thank you, my dear boy."

With these words still ringing in his ear, Frank
was taken away by the thoughtful Mr. Egglestone,
and compelled to lie down.

"You must not agitate the old man, and you need
repose yourself, Frank. I fear the effects of all this
excitement, together with that wound, on your slender
constitution."

"O, my wound is nothing!" Frank declared. "See
that he and Atwater have every thing done for them
— won't you, Mr. Egglestone?"

The minister promised, and Frank endeavored to
settle his mind to rest.

But he could not sleep. Every five minutes he
started up to inquire after his friends. Hour after
hour passed, and he still remained wakeful as a spirit
doomed never to sleep again. His wounded arm
pained him; and he had so many things to think
of, — his suffering comrades, old Buckley shot out of
the tree, his rebel brother, his folks at home, and all
the whirling incidents and horrors of that dread day.

So he thought, and thought; and prayed silently
for the old drummer groaning on his bed of pain;
and pleaded for Atwater lying there, still, with the

death-shadow he had foreseen darkening the portal of his body. And Frank longed for his mother, as he grew weary and weak, until at last sleep came in mercy, and dropped her soft, vapory veil over his soul.

The thrilling news of the victory came north by telegraph. Then followed letters from correspondents, giving details of the battle, when, one morning, Helen Manly ran home in a glow of excitement, bringing a damp and crumpled newspaper.

"News from Frank!" she cried, out of breath.

In a moment the little family was gathered about her, the parents eager and pale.

"Is he living? Tell me that!" said Mrs. Manly.

"Yes, but he has been wounded, and is in the hospital."

"Wounded!" broke forth Mr. Manly in consternation; but his wife kept her soul in silence, waiting with compressed white lips to learn more.

"In the arm — not badly. There is a whole half column about him here. For he has made himself famous — Frank! our dear, dear Frank!" And the quick tears flooding the girl's eyes fell upon the paper.

Mrs. Manly snatched the sheet and read, how her boy had distinguished himself; how he had captured a rebel, and fought gallantly in the ranks, and received a wound without minding it; and how all who had witnessed his conduct, both officers and men, were praising him; it was all there — in the newspaper.

"What adds to the romance of this boy's story," said the writer in conclusion, "is a circumstance which occurred at the capture of the breastwork. Among the dead and wounded left behind when the enemy took to flight, was a rebel captain, of northern parentage, who came south a few years ago, married a southern belle, became a slaveholder, joined the slaveholders' rebellion in consequence, and lost his life in defence of Roanoke Island. He lived long enough to recognize in the drummer boy *his own younger brother*, and died in his arms."

Great was the agitation into which the family was thrown by this intelligence.

"O that I had the wings of a dove!" said Mrs. Manly. "For I must go, I must go to my child!"

Pride and joy in his youthful heroism, pain and grief for the other's tragic end, all was absorbed in the dreadful uncertainty which hung about the welfare of the favorite son; and she knew that not all the attentions and praises of men could make up to him, there on his sick bed, for the absence of his mother.

The family waited, however, — in what anguish of

suspense need not be told, — until the next mail brought them letters from Mr. Egglestone and Captain Edney. By these, their worst fears were confirmed. Exposure, fatigue, excitement, the wound he had received, had done their work with Frank. He was dangerously ill with a fever.

"O, dear!" groaned Mr. Manly, "this wicked, this wicked rebellion! George is killed, and now Frank! What can we do? what can we do, mother?" he asked, helplessly.

While he was groaning, his wife rose up with that energy which so often atoned for the lack of it in him.

"I am going to Roanoke Island! I am going to my child in the hospital!"

That very day she set out. Alone she went, but she was not long without a companion. On the boat to Fortress Monroe she saw a solitary and disconsolate young woman, whose face she was confident of having seen somewhere before. She accosted her, found her going the same journey with herself, and on a similar errand, and learned her history.

"My husband, that I was married to at the cars just as his regiment was leaving Boston, has been shot at Roanoke Island, and whether he is alive or dead I do not know!"

"Your husband," said Mrs. Manly, — "my son knows him well. They were close friends!"

And from that moment the mother of Frank and the wife of Atwater were close friends also, supporting and consoling each other on the journey.

XXXIII.

A FRIEND IN NEED.

AT Roanoke Island, a certain tall, lank, athletic private had been detailed for fatigue duty at the landing, when the steamer from the inlet arrived.

Being at leisure, he was watching with an expression of drollery and inquisitiveness for somebody to tell him the news, when he saw two bewildered, anxious women come ashore, and look about them, as if waiting for assistance.

Prompted by his naturally accommodating disposition, and no less by honest curiosity, the soldier stepped up to them.

"Ye don't seem over'n above familiar in these parts, ladies," he said, with his politest grin.

"We are looking for an officer who promised to aid us in finding our friends in the hospital — or at least in getting news from them," said the elder of the two, — a fine-looking, though distressed and care-worn woman of forty.

"Sho! wal I s'pose he's got other things to look.

after, like as not!" And the soldier, in his sympathy, cast his eyes around in search of the officer. "Got friends in the hospital, hev ye?" Then peering curiously under the bonnet of the young female, "Ain't you the gal that merried Atwater?"

"O! do you know him? Is he — is he alive?" By which eager interrogatives he perceived that she was "the gal."

The droll countenance grew solemn. "I ain't edzac'ly prepared to answer that last question, Miss — Miss Atwater!" he said, with some embarrassment. "But the fust I can respond to with right good will. Did I know him!" — Tears came into his eyes as he added, "Abe Atwater, ma'am, was my friend; and a braver soldier or a better man don't at this moment exist!"

"Then you must know my boy, too!" cried the elder female, — "Frank Manly, drummer."

The soldier brightened at once.

"Frank Manly! 'Whom not to know argues one's self unknown.' Your most obedient, ma'am," — bowing and scraping. "Your son has attracted the attention of the officers, and made himself pop'lar with every body. Mabby ye haven't heerd ——"

"I've heard," interrupted the anxious mother. "But how is he? Tell me that!"

"Wal, he was a little grain more chirk last night,

I was told. He has had a fever, and been delirious, and all that — perty nigh losing his chance o' bein' promoted, he was, one spell! But now I guess his life's about as sure's his commission, which Cap'n Edney says there ain't no doubt about."

"So young!" said Mrs. Manly, trembling with interest.

"He's young, but he's got what we want in officers — that is, sperit; he's chock full of that. I take some little pride in him myself," added the private. "We was almost like brothers, me and Frank was! 'In the desert, in the battle, in the ocean-tempest's wrath, we stood together, side by side; one hope was ours, one path!'"

"This, then, is Seth Tucket!" exclaimed Mrs. Manly, who knew him by his poetry.

"That's my name, ma'am, at your service!" And Seth made another tremendous bow. "But I see," he said, "you're anxious; ye want to git to the hospital. I tell ye, Frank 'll be glad to see ye; he used to rave about you in his delirium; he would call 'mother! mother!' sometimes half the night."

"Poor child! poor, dear child!" said Mrs. Manly. "I can't wait! help me, sir, — show me the way to him, if nothing more!"

"Hello!" shouted Seth. "Whose cart is this? Where's the driver of this cart? It's been standin'

here this hour, and nobody owns it." He jumped into
it. "Who claims this vehicle? 'Who so base as
would not help a woman? If any, speak! for him have
I offended!' Nobody? Then I take the responsibility
— and the cart too! Hop in, ladies! Here's a board
for you to set on. I'll drive ye to the hospital, and
bring back the kerridge before Uncle Sam misses it."

The women were only too glad to accept the invitation, and they were soon seated on the board. Seth
adjusted his anatomy to the edge of the cart-box, and
drove off. But he soon stood up, declaring that a
hungry fellow like him couldn't stand that board, — he
was too sharp set.

Mrs. Manly did not venture to ask again about Atwater, — what he had already said of him having gone
so heavily to the poor wife's heart. But she could
inquire about the old drum-major, who, she had heard,
was wounded.

"Old Sinjin? Wal! I'm in jest the same dilemmy
consarning him as Atwater. They've both been sick
and at the pint of death ever sence the fight. Now
one of 'em's dead, and t'other's alive. A chap that was
at the hospital told me this morning, 'One of them
sickest fellers in your regiment died last night,' says
he; 'I don't know which of 'em,' says he. And I
haven't had a chance yet to find out."

"O, haste then!" cried the young wife. "May be
my husband is living still!"

"Shouldn't wonder the least might if he is," said Seth, willing to encourage her. "For he has hung on to life wonderfully; he said he believed you was coming, and he couldn't bear the idee of dying before he could see you once more. Old Buckley's bullet has been found, you'll be pleased to know."

"Old Buckley? Who is old Buckley?"

"The Maryland secessionist that shot your husband, and that I brought down from the tree to pay for it. He never 'll git into another tree, without his soul goes into a gobble-turkey, as I should think it might, and flies up in one to roost!"

"And the bullet!——"

"As I was going to tell ye, it's been found. It went through the Bible that you gave him (and that Frank's preserving for you now, I believe), and lodged in his body, the doctor couldn't tell where. But one night Mr. Egglestone,— the fighting minister, you know, that married you, — he was bathing Abe's back, and what did he find but a bunch, that Abe said was sore. 'Doctor!' says he, 'I've found the bullet!' And, sure enough! the doctor come and cut out the lead. It had gone clean through the poor feller, — into his breast, and out under his side!—Hello!" said Seth, "I shall hev to turn out and wait for that company to march by. I swan to man ef 'tain't my company, — or a part on't, at least! They're drum-

21

ming out a coward, to the tune of the *Rogue's March!*"

The women were all impatience to get on; and Mrs. Manly felt but the faintest gleam of interest in the procession, until, as it drew near, in a wretched figure, wearing, in place of the regimental uniform, a suit of rags that might have been taken from some contraband, with drummers before and fixed bayonets behind, she recognized — Jack Winch!

"Wal!" said Seth, "I'd ruther go into a fight and be shot dead than go out of camp in that style! See that label, 'COWARD,' on his back? But he deserves it, ef ever a chap did!"

And Seth, as he drove on, related the story of Jack's miserable boasting and poltroonery. Much as she pitied the wretch, Mrs. Manly could not help remembering his treachery towards her son, and feeling that Frank was now amply avenged.

XXXIV.

THE HOSPITAL.

LET us pass on before, and take a peep into the hospital. There we find Ned Ellis, playing dominoes with one hand, and joking to keep up the spirits of his companions. There lies Frank on his cot, with blanched countenance, eyes closed, and pale lips smiling, as if in dreams. Of his two friends, Atwater and the old drummer, only one, as Seth Tucket said, remains. One was carried out last night — in a coffin his cold form is laid — life's fitful fever is over with him.

And the other? Very still, very pale, stretched on his narrow bed, no motion of breathing perceptible, behold him! What is it we see in that sculptured, placid face? Is it life, or is it death? It's neither life nor death, but sleep, that dim gulf between.

Mr. Egglestone, who has been much about the hospital from the first, enters with a radiant look, and steps lightly to Frank's side.

The drummer boy's eyes unclose, and smile their welcome.

(323)

"Better, still better, I am glad to see!" says the minister, cheerily.

"Almost well," answered Frank, although so weak that he can hardly speak. "I shall be out again in a day or two. The fever has quite left me; and I was having such a beautiful dream. I thought I was a water-lily, floating on a lake; and the lake, they told me, was *sleep;* and I felt all whiteness and peace! Wasn't it pretty?"

"Pretty, and true too!" said the minister, with a suffusing tear, as he looked at the pale, gentle boy, and thought how much like a white fragrant lily he was. "I have news for you, Frank. The steamer has arrived."

"O! and letters?"

"Probably, though I have none yet. But something besides letters!"—Mr. Egglestone whispered confidentially, "Atwater's wife is here!"

"Is she? Brave girl!—O, dear!" said Frank, his features changing suddenly, "why didn't my mother come too! She might, I think! It seems as if I couldn't wait, as if I couldn't live, till I see her!"

"Well, Frank," then said the minister, having thus prepared him, "your mother did think — your mother is here!"

At the moment, Mrs. Manly, who could be no longer restrained, flew to the bedside of her son. He started up with a wild cry; she caught him in her arms; they clung and kissed and cried together.

"Mother! mother!" "My child! my darling child!" were the only words that could be heard in that smothering embrace.

Mr. Egglestone turned, and took the hand of her companion, who had entered with her, and led her to the cot where lay the still figure and placid, sculptured face. O woman, be strong! O wife, be calm! keep back the tears, stifle the anguish, of that heaving breast.

She is strong, she is calm, tears and anguish are repressed. She bends over the scarcely breathing form, gazes into the utterly pallid face, and with clasped hands in silence blesses him, prays for him — her husband.

For this is he — Abe Atwater, the shadow of death he foresaw still darkening the portal of his body, as if hesitating to enter, nor yet willing to pass by. And the face in the coffin outside there is the face of the old drummer, whose soul, let us hope, is at peace. One was taken — will the other be left?

The eyes of Abe opened; they beheld the vision of his wife, and gladness, like a river of soft waters, glides into his soul. O, may it be a river of life to him! As love has held his spirit back from death, so may its power restore him; for such things have been; and there is no medicine for the sick body or sinking soul like the breath and magnetic touch of love.

Frank meanwhile was lying on his bed, holding his mother's hands, and drinking in the joy of her presence. And she was feeding his rapture with the tenderest motherly words and looks, and telling him of home.

"But how selfish 1 am!" said Frank. "How little you could afford to leave, and come here! I thought I was going to be a help to you, and, the best I can do, I am only a trouble and a hinderance!"

"I could not stop an instant to think of trouble or expense when my darling was in danger!" exclaimed the grateful mother. "I feel that God will take care of us; if we are his children, he will provide for all our wants. Will he not, Mr. Egglestone?"

"When I have read to you this paper," replied the minister, "then you can be the judge. I was requested to read it to Frank as soon as he was able to hear it — after his friend's death."

"Is it something for me? Poor old Mr. Sinjin!" exclaimed Frank. "He died last night, mother. But he was so happy, and so willing to go, I can't mourn for him. What is the paper?"

"A few nights ago he requested me to come to his side and write as he should dictate." And the clergyman, seating himself, read: —

" 'The Last Will and Testament of Servetus St. John, commonly called Old Sinjin.

" 'I, Servetus St. John, Drummer, being of sound mind, but of body fast failing unto death, having received its mortal hurt in battle for my country, do give and bequeath of my possessions as follows: —

" '*Item.* My Soul I return to the Maker who gave it, and my Flesh to the dust whence it came.

" '*Item.* To my Country and the Cause of Freedom, as I have given my last poor services, so I likewise give cheerfully my Life.

" '*Item.* To Mehitabel Craig, my only surviving sister after the flesh, I give what alone she can claim of me, and what, as a dying sinner, I have no right to withhold, my full pardon for all offences.

" '*Item.* To my present friend and comforter, Mr. Egglestone, as a memento of my deep obligations to him, I give my watch.

" '*Item.* To my fellow-sufferer, Abram Atwater, or to his widow, in case of his decease, I bequeath the sum of one hundred dollars.

" '*Item.* To my fellow-sufferer and dearly beloved pupil, Frank Manly, I give, in token of affection, a miniature which will be found after my death.

" '*Item.* To the same Frank Manly I also give and bequeath the residue of all my worldly possessions, to wit : — ' "

Then followed an enumeration of certain stocks and deposits, amounting to the sum of three thousand dollars.

The will was duly witnessed, and Mr. Egglestone was the appointed executor.

Frank was silent; he was crying, with his hands over his face.

"So you see, my young friend," said Mr. Egglestone, "you have, for your own comfort, and for the benefit of your good parents, a snug little fortune, which you will come into possession of in due time. As for the miniature, I may as well hand it to you now. I found it after the old man's death. He always wore it on his heart."

He took it from its little soiled buckskin sheath, and gave it to Mrs. Manly. She turned pale as she looked at it. Frank was eager to see it, and, almost reluctantly, she placed it in his hands. It might almost have passed for a portrait of himself, only it was that of a girl; and he knew at once that it was his mother, as she had looked at his age.

While he was gazing at the singular memento of the old man's romantic and undying attachment, Mrs. Manly looked away, with the air of one resolutely turning her mind from one painful subject to another.

"I wish to ask you, Mr. Egglestone, what dispo-

sition has been made of —— I had another son,
you know."

He understood her.

"I trust," said he, "that what Captain Edney and
myself thought proper to do will meet your approval.
After the battle, the wife of Captain Manly sent a
request to have his body forwarded to her by a flag
of truce. We consulted Frank, who told us to do as
we pleased about it. Accordingly, we obtained permission to grant her request, and the body of her
husband was sent to her."

There was for a moment a look, as of one who felt
bitter wrong, on Mrs. Manly's face; but it passed.

"You did well, Mr. Egglestone. To her who had
got the soul belonged the body also. May peace go
with it to her desolated home!"

"Mother!" whispered Frank, gazing still at the
miniature, "tell me! am I right? do I know now
why it was the dear old man thought so much of
me?"

"If you have not guessed, my child, I will tell you.
Years ago, when I was the little girl you see there,
he was good enough to think *I* was good enough to
marry him. That is all."

Frank said no more, but laid the picture on his
heart, — for it was his, and the dearest part of the
dear old man's legacy.

XXXV.

CONCLUSION.

AFTER a long delay Captain Edney came; apologizing for not appearing to welcome his drummer boy's mother and his old schoolmistress before. His excuse was valid: one of his men, S. Tucket by name, had got into a scrape by running off with one of Uncle Sam's carts, and he had been to help him out of it.

He found a new light shining in the hospital — the light of woman's influence; the light of life to Frank and his friend Atwater, nor to them only, but to all upon whom it shone.

Mrs. Manly remained in the hospital until her son was able to travel, when leave of absence was granted him, and all his friends crowded to bid him farewell, as he departed in the boat with his mother for the north — for home!

Of his journey, of his happy arrival, the greetings from father, sister, little brother, friends — of all this I would gladly write a chapter or two; but he is no longer the Drummer Boy now, and so our business with him is over. And so he left the service? Not he.

"I'm to be a Soldier Boy now!" he declared to all those who came to shake him by the hand and hear his story from his own lips.

His wound was soon healed, and he hastened to return to his regiment; for he was eager to be learning every thing belonging to the profession of a soldier. It was not long, however, before he came north again — this time on surprising business. Captain Edney, who had won the rank of Colonel at the battle of Newbern, had been sent home to raise a regiment; and he had been permitted to choose from his own company such persons as he thought best fitted to assist him, and hold commissions under him.

He chose Gray, Seth Tucket, and Frank. Another of our friends afterwards joined the regiment, with the rank of First Lieutenant; having quite recovered from his wound, under the tender nursing of his wife.

With his friends Edney, Gray, Tucket, and At-water, Frank was as happy as ever a young officer in a new service could be. He began as second lieutenant; but ——

But here our story must end; for to relate how he has fought his way up, step by step, to a rank which was never more fairly earned, would require a separate volume, — materials for which we may possibly find some day in his own letters to his mother, and in those of Colonel Edney to his sister Helen.

———————

Some extracts from a letter just received from the hero of these pages may perhaps interest the reader.

"I cannot tell you, sir, how much astonished I was on opening the package you sent me. I don't think the mysterious bundle that contained the watch dear old 'Mr. St. John' gave me surprised me half as much. I had never seen any *proof-sheets* before, and hardly knew what to make of them at first. Then you should have heard me scream at Gray and Atwater. 'Boys,' says I, 'here's a story founded on our adventures!' I sat up all that night reading it, and I must confess I had to blush a good many times before I got through. I see you have not called any of us by our real names; but I soon found out who 'Abe,' and 'Seth,' and 'Jack Winch,' and all the other characters are meant for. I have read ever so many pages to 'Seth' himself, and he has laughed as heartily as any of us over his own oddities. We all wonder how you could have written the story, giving all the circumstances, and even the conversations that took place, so correctly; ut I remember, when I was at your house, you kept me talking, and wrote down nearly every thing I said; besides which, I find there was a good deal more in my journal and letters than I supposed, when I consented to let you have them and make what use of them you pleased. Little did I think then, that ever such a book as the 'Drummer Boy.' could be made out of them.

"You ask me to point out any important errors I may notice, in order that you may correct them before the book is published. Well, the night the row was in camp, when the 'Blues' cut down the captain's tent, the company was ordered out, and the roll called, and three other fellows put under guard, before Abe and I were let off. I might mention two or three similar mistakes, but I consider them too trifling to speak of. There are, besides, two or three omissions, which struck me in reading the wind-up of the story. 'Jack Winch' went home, and died of a fever within a month. If it isn't too late, I wish you would put that in; for I think it shows that those who think most of saving their lives are sometimes the first to lose them.

"You might add, too, that 'Mr. Egglestone' is now the chaplain of our regiment. We all love him, and he is doing a great deal of good here. I have put the 'Drummer Boy' into his hands, and I just saw him laughing over it. If every body reads it with the interest we do here in camp, it will be a great success. . . .

"There is another thing — but this you need not put into the book. With the money my dear old friend and master left me, I have bought the house our folks live in, so that, whatever happens to me, they will never be without a home. . . .

"In conclusion, let me say that, while you have told some things of me I would rather every body should forget, you have, on the whole, given me a much better character than I deserve.

"We are already beginning to call each other by the names you have given us, and I take great pleasure in subscribing myself,

    "Yours, truly,

       "FRANK MANLY."

www.ingramcontent.com/pod-product-compliance
Lightning Source LLC
Chambersburg PA
CBHW021115270326
41929CB00009B/891